THE
VIEW FROM
THE ROCKING
CHAIR

by Matt McGee

SONRISE MOUNTAIN RANCH

The View From the Rocking Chair
Copyright © 2013 by Matt McGee

This title is available at www.sonrisemountainranch.org.

Requests for information should be addressed to:
PO Box 220
Cimarron, CO 81220

All Scripture quotations, unless otherwise indicated, are taken from The Holy Bible: New International Version Translation, Copyright © 1984.

ISBN 978-1-4675-8812-6 (paperback)
First Edition 2013
Printed in the United States of America

Editing: Suzanne Gosselin
Additional Editorial Work: Jeff Oraker, Nic Scherer, and Chee-Hwa Cole
Cover and Interior Design: Melissa Tenpas
Cover Photography: iStockPhoto® (front) and Maddison McGee (back)

This book is dedicated to my God, my wife, and my children.

First, to the One who has shown me amazing grace in rescuing me from myself and perfect faithfulness in guiding me to a place where I can invest in what matters most—this is for Your purposes.

Soli Deo Gloria.

Next, to my bride Chantal—you are a magnificent partner, helper, prayer warrior, lover, Bible teacher, and traveling buddy on this remarkable journey. Thank you for sacrificing and persevering each day.

Finally, to Maddison, Abby Grace, Rebekah, Eden, Zeke, and Viv Joy—you are a priceless treasure. It is such a joy to be with you and to love and serve others alongside you. Your lives teach and inspire me. Thanks for being gracious with your Dad.

Special thanks to Suzanne Gosselin, Jeff Oraker, Nic Scherer, Chee-Hwa Cole, and Melissa Tenpas for your excellent editorial and design work. Thanks to Val Drown for your multi-faceted assistance in this project. Thanks to Lance McDowell, Jerry McGee, Allison Scherer, and Kathy Carnahan for the encouragement and prayer. Thank you to the Sonrise Board for helping bring this to fruition. Thank you Mom and Dad for your example that has given me strength.

TABLE OF CONTENTS

USING THIS BOOK AS A SMALL GROUP RESOURCE

We have included review and small group questions at the end of each chapter so this book can be read, studied, and discussed with a small group or Sunday School class. Here are two reading plans that can be used with a group:

15-WEEK OR 15-SESSION PLAN

Read one chapter each week (or session) and answer the small group questions before the meeting. Discuss the questions and any exercises in the chapter during the group meeting.

6-WEEK OR 6-SESSION PLAN

This plan may be preferable for groups that meet once or twice a month. Read the designated chapters and answer the small group questions before each meeting. Discuss selected questions and key exercises in the chapter(s) during the group meeting.

Week/Session 1: Introduction and Chapters 1 – 2

Week/Session 2: Chapters 3–5

Week/Session 3: Chapters 6–8

Week/Session 4: Chapters 9–11

Week/Session 5: Chapters 12–14

Week/Session 6: Chapter 15

This plan can be easily lengthened to 8, 10, or 12 weeks per session.

"I WISH I HAD THOUGHT ABOUT THIS TWENTY YEARS AGO."

How many times have I heard these words? Sometimes twenty is replaced by ten, thirty, or forty, but the expression is not uncommon. Each time I hear these words, they bring me joy and sadness. Joy because the speaker sees more clearly now than before, and life ahead promises to be different; sadness because he or she cannot rewrite history or regain all that has been lost.

My wife and I have the privilege of working at a family retreat center in the mountains of Colorado. We get a chance to stand alongside people, often husbands and wives—fathers and mothers— as they take a "time out" to look at their lives.

During the process of making friends with hundreds of people from around the country, we have witnessed many who find themselves in a place that is very different from where they were originally heading. Certainly there are some who find themselves solidly on course. But most feel life is working out differently than they had planned.

We have listened to multitudes of husbands and wives say, "How did we get here?" Or, "This is almost the exact opposite of what we were hoping for." Or, "We've been drifting off course and I've been too busy to see it."

My wife and I both flew airplanes in the Air Force for a number of years. We learned firsthand there are a variety of things that can cause you to get off course when you are flying. Unknown winds can blow you off track. Bad weather can necessitate a detour. Other air traffic can force you to change your flight path. Even your own inattention or distraction can cause you to drift off course.

> HOW DID WE GET HERE? THIS IS ALMOST THE EXACT OPPOSITE OF WHAT WE WERE HOPING FOR.

When we spend time with couples and families on retreat, they share about some of the things that have gotten them off course. Like the winds at high altitudes, busyness seems to be a constant force pushing against families. For others, starting a business or pursuing other career dreams have nudged them off course. The intensity of having and caring for children, especially multiple small children, has caused some families to falter. And still others have been pushed off track by unexpected health problems.

When someone makes a dramatic change in his or her direction in life, it is easy to see. If your next door neighbor, who is a longtime accountant, picks up his family and moves to Vegas, enrolls with his wife in a seven card stud crash course, and sets the family sights on winning the World Series of Poker, everyone knows he has made a 90-degree heading change. He has made a hard left turn and intentionally aimed for a very different destination. But much more common is the phenomena of families subtly drifting off course.

When you are flying an airplane and you begin to slowly drift off course 10 degrees to one side, you normally do not notice this drift if you are looking out the cockpit windows. A gradual 10-degree heading change is virtually imperceptible unless you are looking at the flight instruments. But the end result of such a small course change is surprising and significant.

Let's imagine you are flying on a jet leaving New York for an anniversary celebration with your spouse in southern Italy. You have learned a little of the Italian language and are dreaming about the wonderful food and balmy Mediterranean weather. Shortly after takeoff, the aircraft drifts off course 10 degrees to the South (your right). The pilot is not paying close attention and consequently never discovers the plane has drifted off course.

After flying the appropriate duration, the pilot finds a suitable runway and lands the airplane. When you deplane, you are greeted not by the sights and sounds you expected but by seventy mile an hour winds, forcing sand into your eyes, nose, and ears. Instead of hearing some of the Italian language, you hear Arabic and see camels in the distance. You recognize your dream vacation may be a little different than expected since you are not in southern Italy but rather in the Sahara desert of western Libya.

If you end up in a different destination than planned on your anniversary vacation, you would find it difficult. But that difficulty pales in comparison to ending up in a different destination in *life*. Finding yourself off course, even by a small margin, and doing nothing about it will lead you to a different destination than you desire.

This realization of being "off course" may come to you like an unexpected flash of lightning. Sometimes, it is a husband saying to his wife, "I don't think I love you anymore." Other times it is the accidental discovery of a teenager's secret and destructive lifestyle. But for most, the recognition is not so abrupt and shocking. Because the drift has been slow and gradual, most people can only determine if they are off course after they have left their normal pace and routine for several days.

Only with an unhurried, careful examination can they see if their direction has truly changed. When they do see clearly, many experience the realization they are being directed by "the tyranny of the urgent" rather than by their core values.

Some families may realize that their lifestyle looks and feels just like their neighbors who are not trying to follow God. One father described his drifting off course this way:

In isolating ourselves from church and church people, we sought a simpler faith, away from all the "fakeness" sometimes associated with "religion." But in so doing, I let my thought process become influenced more by the world. Jesus' words and the other truths of the Bible became obscured and pushed into the background...not completely gone, just well off into the periphery of our lives.

Our retreat woke me up. My metaphor is this. At one point in our marriage I was vigilant and studious, working hard to understand God's design for us, and my responsibilities as a husband and a father. I was as diligent as I might be when driving at night; tired, but concerned about the precious cargo in the car—my family. And after a time, I became tired as I struggled to stay awake, and eventually nodded off...only to awaken in a panic, not sure how long I had been asleep at the wheel.

For me, the retreat was one of those moments. I realized I had been asleep at the wheel. My focus had not been on God and His instruction manual for life. Instead, I fell back to philosophy, reason, and morality...thinking that my "superior logical intellect" had mostly everything figured out already. My prayer is that I'll never put myself or my family in that kind of jeopardy again.

Realizing we are off course in life should not cause us to despair, or enter denial or depression. If we are truly off course, it is immensely valuable to recognize it. What matters most is what we do with that knowledge.

If we have drifted off course, even just ten degrees, it is critical that we make a course correction. The destination we will reach at the end of our lives depends upon it. The long-lasting impact your life has on your loved ones depends upon it. What you will honestly be able to say about your life as you look in the mirror depends upon it.

This book is meant to keep you from saying, "I wish I had thought about this *twenty years ago*." It's meant to keep you from having regret due to your choices. If you keep reading, you will have the chance to consider this (what you'll wish you had thought about later) *now*. We will present the thoughts and ideas that generate this sentiment after a retreat.

In this book, we don't promise, "If you do this, your outcome will be exactly that." *But*, if you walk through this book, you can look at the outcomes of life, knowing you tried to make careful, thoughtful, and intentional choices with your eyes focused on what was most important. Are you ready? ▪

CHAPTER ONE

THE VIEW FROM THE ROCKING CHAIR

Show me, Lord, my life's end and the number of my days.

— King David

Imagine yourself on the deck of a log cabin nestled in the Rocky Mountains. You are watching a summer sunset light up a spectacular vista spread out before you. You are sitting in a rocking chair, occasionally rocking back and forth, soaking in the magnificent scenery and marveling at how the setting sunlight transforms the scene before you every five minutes. It is perfectly quiet.

While you are in good health, you are in your eighties, so you know that you have lived the lion's share of your life already. As you take in the sunset, you note the parallel in your own life—you are indeed in the sunset of your days here on earth.

You begin to think back over your eight plus decades of life and honestly evaluate what you have lived for, what you have invested your life in, and how you have spent your time, your energy, and your money.

As you sit in that rocking chair, **what will you care about most? What will you not care about at all?** Don't rush past this. Carefully consider these questions. Take a few minutes and make a list.

- my family
- that my children know God + God's word
- memories of laughing

not @ material things

If we have the opportunity someday to sit and honestly evaluate our lives—to truthfully assess what we have poured our lives into and what we have chosen to say "no" to—there are two things that are probably clear even now.

First, nobody wants to look back over the choices he has made and end up filled with regret. None of us want to experience the knot in our stomach, the deep dread coming from the realization that we wasted our lives on things that are meaningless to us at the end.

Second, all of us want to sit in that rocking chair able to say, "Thank you, God. You did it. You helped me truly live for the things that matter most to me now and that will matter for all eternity."

Most likely, we all desire to be filled with gratitude to God for His faithfulness in guiding us and the all-encompassing joy and peace that comes from knowing we faithfully fulfilled our role—not perfectly, but faithfully.

One of the goals for this book is to help you get to the rocking chair without regrets and instead filled with gratitude, joy, and peace because you lived for the things that matter most. To accomplish this goal, we must help you develop clear vision for what you will care about at the end of your life.

WHAT *WILL* YOU CARE ABOUT AT THE END?

We have a family friend who works as a nurse in an oncology ward and regularly spends time with those who are terminally ill. During a discussion on what people care about, she said, "This is what people talk about when they know they don't have much time left. They tell me to spend time with my family, cherish my kids, and love my husband. They know what matters so they tell me how I should live."

These patients declare what many people can see long before they reach the end of their lives—**relationships will be more important than everything else.**

Throughout the Bible, God gives us vision for what we will care about at the end of our lives. When the apostle Paul writes to the believers in Thessalonica (modern-day Greece), we get a good look:

"For what is our hope, our joy, or the crown in which we will glory in the presence of our Lord Jesus when He comes? Is it not you? Indeed, you are our glory and joy."
—1 Thessalonians 2:19-20

Notice what *will not be* our crown, our joy, our glory as we one day stand before the Lord. There is no mention of a beautiful house with attractive landscaping, becoming executive vice-president, taking exotic vacations, or winning first-place ribbons. These are not evil accomplishments; they are simply not what we will be thinking about at the end.

What will be our crown and our joy, our hope and our glory before the Lord? People. The lives of people with whom we have shared life and have had meaningful relationships. We will be thinking about our spouses, our children, friends, co-workers, and others we have had the chance to know and love. We will care about these questions: What was the quality of my relationship with them? How well did I love them? Was I faithful to point them to the Lord and a life of eternal purpose? Will I be with them in Heaven forever and ever?

God provides vision for us, not only in His Word, but also in our innate longings as beings created in His image. God has embedded certain truths, abilities, and realities in our DNA—at the core of who we are. God has graciously endowed all people with a sense of what will be most important at the end of their lives.

As I speak with the many men and women who attend our retreats and conferences, as well as others, it is remarkable how consistently people with varied backgrounds and beliefs accurately identify what will matter most at the end of their lives. Unfortunately, this sense can be corrupted, weakened, or forgotten. In addition, having a sense of what will matter most at the end does not ensure that we will make decisions in light of that knowledge. So while God has designed us with this innate sense of what we should care about, quite often we do not appear to consult this sense as we make choices.

In this book, we hope to heighten and hone that sense and provide a means for you to make all your choices from clear, God-given vision for your life.

THINKING ABOUT THE END

From my observations, most people do not *regularly think about* what they will care about at the end of their lives. The normal pace most of us live at does not provide much time for introspection or promote thinking about things that seem far down the road of life. The incessant demands and commitments of daily life lead us into the "tyranny of the urgent" where deep introspection is rare.

In many cases, it takes a jarring life event or tragedy to cause us to think about what will matter most to us at the end of our lives. Attending a funeral or hearing about the death of a family member or close friend can do this. The words, "You have cancer," may shift our focus. Even the birth of a child can be a wake-up call. All of these instances can cause us to think about our mortality and the deeper meaning of our lives. But the impact of these events on our thinking is often short-lived. We quickly return to a perspective where thinking six months down the road is long-range planning.

Not long ago, I attended the funeral of a friend killed in a plane crash. At the funeral, I had a chance to visit with numerous friends who I had not seen for almost a decade. Because of the setting, many of them wanted to talk about the most significant things in their lives: their marriages, their relationships with their kids, where their lives were headed, what they thought about God. In that moment, they were not focused on their awards, titles, or salaries.

In the weeks and months following the funeral, however, as I attempted to continue some of those conversations, the response was less than encouraging. The desire to talk about the things that matter most had faded away.

RELOCATING OUR POINT OF VIEW

The Bible talks about looking back on your life from the end as a means of making wise decisions today. Psalm 39 is one of many instances where the writer reaches through the fog of difficult and confusing circumstances, searching for clearer perspective. Note where the psalmist finds the enhanced point of view:

"Show me, Lord, my life's end and the number of my days; let me know how fleeting my life is." —Psalm 39:4

Next, consider what has been referred to as the "Hall of Faith" in Hebrews 11. The author of Hebrews assembles a congregation of Old Testament heroes, some we would expect to see and some we would not. They are heroes not because they were perfect. Jacob deceived, David murdered, Rahab prostituted, and Samson fornicated—but they are on the list.

They are heroes not because their lives had storybook endings. Some were stoned, sawed in two, or put to death by the sword. Others were destitute, wandered in deserts, and lived in caves and holes in the ground.

Verse 13 reveals the reason this varied group of people made this prestigious list: *"All these people were still living by faith when they died."*

They persevered in their faith until the end. What allowed them to do this? They lived with the future in mind. They are described this way:

> " . . . *looking forward to the city . . . whose architect and builder is God."*

> *"They admitted that they were aliens and strangers on earth."*

> *"They were longing for a better country—a heavenly one."*

> " . . . *chose to be mistreated along with the people of God rather than to enjoy the pleasures of sin for a short time."*

> " . . . *regarded disgrace for the sake of Christ as of greater value than the treasures of Egypt, because he was looking ahead to his reward."*

They considered the future, and at some momentous point in their lives, determined *to make their decisions based on the "destination" they were aiming for.*

Living with the end in view even gained this group of God-followers a sort of epitaph:

> *"God is not ashamed to be called their God . . . He has prepared a city for them . . . the world was not worthy of them."*

What an amazing thing to have recorded as your legacy.

When we look at Jesus' life, we find Him regularly teaching His followers about living with the future in view. In Matthew 6, He challenges them to give to the poor, pray, and fast in secret for the Lord alone instead of for the applause and admiration of people. He challenges them to be motivated by a future rewards from their heavenly Father rather than the immediate reward they receive from people.

He even challenges their future versus immediate perspective on the most difficult of issues—material possessions—when He says, *"Do not store up for yourselves treasures on earth, where moth and rust destroy . . . But store up for yourselves treasures in heaven, where moth and rust do not destroy . . . "* —Matthew 6:19-20 Jesus sought to relocate his disciples' decision-making point of view to the end of their lives.

Paul does the same.

> *"Forgetting what is behind and straining toward what is ahead, I press on toward the goal to win the prize for which God has called me heavenward in Christ Jesus. All of us who are mature should take such a view of things . . . Join with others in following my example, brothers, and take note of those who live according to the pattern we gave you."*
> —Philippians 3:13-15, 17

Paul passionately exhorts the family of God to drive ahead with our future destination in focus. Live today with the end in view.

INTENTIONAL LIVING

The view from the rocking chair can be a clarifying force in our lives. If you are able to keep in mind the things you will care about most at the end of your life, there will be purpose and consistency as you develop plans and make daily choices.

Intentional living is having a purpose, a direction toward an object; it is pointing toward some target or state of affairs. We all have some level of intention in our day-to-day decisions. We correct our kids, call a friend, go to the gym, and make dinner, all while having an objective in mind for each activity. But many of us struggle to consistently line up all our choices toward the same overarching objective. We tend to make choices aimed at a broad array of seemingly unrelated objectives. This produces an internal sense and outward appearance of being scattered.

If we're honest with ourselves, most of us find little satisfaction living this way. The view from the rocking chair can help us align our choices so that they are clearly connected and tangibly moving us toward a desirable outcome.

Here's an example of what I'm talking about. Every professional football player wants to win the Super Bowl. He dreams of ending his season standing on a platform, being showered with confetti, and holding the Lombardi trophy while his fans cheer wildly and 100 million people watch on television. Every player has that target in his sights for the other 364 days of the year.

So each day, he wakes at 6 a.m., drinks a protein shake, stretches for thirty minutes, and lifts weights for two hours. The rest of his day is filled with team meetings, film study, practice, time with a personal trainer, and an abundance of performance-enhancing food and drink. He goes to bed early enough to get up and do it again the next day.

The end goal helps him focus his diet, his schedule, who he spends time with, and how he uses his mental energy. His immanent objective is clear and it shows up in all of his choices. We could live the same way for a purpose and prize that will not fade away. The apostle Paul talked about this.

> "Remember that in a race everyone runs, but only one person gets the prize. You also must run in such a way that you will win. All athletes practice self-control. They do it to win a prize that will fade away, but we do it for an eternal prize. So I run straight to the goal with purpose in every step. I am not like a boxer who misses his punches. I discipline my body like an athlete, training it to do what I should. Otherwise, I fear that after preaching to others I myself might be disqualified."
> —1 Corinthians 9:24-27, NLT

If you choose to aim your life at the things you will care about most in the rocking chair, you can have unwavering intention as you set your sights on the "big picture."

LIVING WITHOUT THE END IN VIEW

What happens when we live without the end of our lives in view? We are prone to select a target that is nearsighted. Time and again, we make decisions we will regret.

Many married people, in a challenging season of life, make decisions keeping only the immediate circumstances in view. For example, a husband and father finds himself in a marriage that is dry, lifeless, and not bringing happiness as it once did. An attractive co-worker comes along, seeming to be everything his spouse is not. The man begins to make bad choices in his thought life and then in his words and actions. Little by little, choice by choice, he moves closer to the edge.

Finally, the secret thoughts of an affair turn into reality. He makes a decision that felt right in the moment. But was it worth it? If he could fast forward his point of view ten or twenty years down the road of life, would he have chosen the same thing?

In their book, *The Language of Love*, Gary Smalley and John Trent share this letter from a 14-year-old girl to her father after he left his family for another woman:

Dear Daddy,

It's late at night, and I'm sitting in the middle of my bed writing to you. I've wanted to talk with you so many times during the past few weeks but there never seems to be any time. Dad, I realize you're dating someone else. And I know you and Mom may never get back together. But I want you at least to understand what's going on in our lives.

Dad, I feel like our family has been riding in a nice car for a long time. But over the years, the car has developed some problems. It's smokes a lot, the wheels wobble, and the seat covers are ripped. The car's been really hard to drive or ride in because of all the shaking and squeaking. But it's still a great automobile—or at least it could be. With a little work, I know it could run for years. Since we got the car, Brian and I have been in the backseat while you and Mom have been up front. We feel really secure with you driving and Mom beside you.

But last month, Mom was at the wheel. It was nighttime, and we had just turned the corner near our house. Suddenly, we all looked up and saw another car, out of control, heading straight for us. Mom tried to swerve out of the way, but the other car smashed into us. The impact sent us flying off the road and crashing into a lamppost. The thing is, Dad, just before we were hit, we could see that you were driving the other car. And we saw something else: Sitting next to you was another woman.

It was such a terrible accident. Mom was really hurt. She was thrown into the steering wheel and broke several ribs. One of them punctured her lungs and almost pierced her heart. Brian was covered with cuts from the broken glass and he shattered his arm, which is now in a cast. He's still in so much pain and shock that he doesn't want to talk or play with anyone. As for me, I was thrown from the car and stuck out in the cold for a long time with my right leg broken.

There have been times since that night when I wondered if any of us would make it. Even though we're getting a little better, we're all still in the hospital. The doctors say I'll need a lot of therapy and I know they can help me get better. But I wish it were you who was helping me, instead of them.

The pain is bad, but what's even worse is that we all miss you so much. My heart would explode with joy if somehow I could look up and see you walk into my room. At night when the hospital is really quiet, they push Brian and me into Mom's room, and we all talk about you. We talk about how much we loved driving with you and how we wish you were with us now.

Daddy, are you all right? Are you hurting from the wreck? Do you need us like we need you? If you need me, I'm here and I love you. Your daughter, Kimberly [1]

We do not have to live with the deep pain and unending regret from nearsighted decisions like this. God desires to give us vision that will help protect us from this reality and guide us in righteous living.

You may think the rocking chair perspective is not as necessary for people who are truly committed to the Lord. The Reverend Billy Graham has been a wonderful example in so many ways. Because of his honesty, we can learn something from his life we might not have expected. In his biography, he reflected on his regrets in an interview:

> *"Although I have much to be grateful for as I look back over my life, I also have many regrets. I have failed many times, and I would do many things differently. For one thing, I would speak less and study more, and I would spend more time with my family. When I look back over the schedule I kept thirty or forty years ago, I am staggered by all the things we did and the engagements we kept. Were all those engagements necessary? Was I as discerning as I might have been about which ones to take and which to turn down? I doubt it. Every day I was absent from my family is gone forever."* [2]

Billy Graham's frank reflection encourages us to adopt the view from the rocking chair so we can make decisions from the best vantage point and steer clear of these kinds of regrets.

What would life be like if every day we thought about what we will care about most at the end of our lives? If every day, we made our choices reflecting the perspective we will have in the rocking chair? What would our lives look like?

We will take this journey together one step at a time. Are you ready for step one?

The first step to living with the rocking chair perspective is an exercise called "The View from the Rocking Chair"—your personal opportunity to carefully consider what you will care about most at the end of your life. You took a brief peek at the beginning of this chapter. Here is a chance to take a good long look down the road.

We want you to carefully consider and write down what you hope those closest to you will say about you at the end of your life. This is not a time to write down what they would say right now. This is a time to dream about what your spouse, children, friends, and the Lord might say about you if everything goes as you would hope from this point forward.

Here is another way to think about it: If the Lord has His way in your life from now until the end, what would those closest to you say about you? It is best to do this exercise with a willingness to put words in the mouths of others. For example, if I am doing this exercise, I write:

At the end of my life my wife, Chantal, will say . . .

- Matt showed me every day that I was first to him, only after God.
- He loved me sacrificially and put my needs before his own.
- He extended forgiveness quickly, graciously, and humbly.
- He was a rock; I could always depend upon him.
- I cannot remember the last time Matt was harsh with me.
- He helped me believe I was beautiful and precious.
- I have trusted and obeyed the Lord more fully because of Matt's life.

My wife, Chantal, could not honestly say all those things about me today. But it is my deep desire and prayer to God that she will be able to say that when I am in the rocking chair.

Take a minute now to fill out "The View From the Rocking Chair" exercise on the next few pages or write these questions down in a journal or on a piece of paper you can hold onto.

Find a time and place where you can be quiet and undistracted for fifteen to thirty minutes. Reread the first paragraph of this chapter. Ask the Lord to help you. Write down your answers to the four questions below (or the ones that are applicable to you). ▪

THE VIEW FROM THE ROCKING CHAIR

At the end of my life, my spouse will say . . .

_____

_____

_____

_____

_____

At the end of my life, my children will say . . .

_____

_____

_____

_____

_____

At the end of my life, my friends will say . . .

_____

_____

_____

_____

_____

At the end of my life, my Lord will say . . .

_____

_____

_____

_____

_____

Go to www.sonrisemountainranch.org/exercises/rocking_chair to download and print this page.

This exercise can affect your life significantly. If you reflect on your answers regularly and keep them in mind when making choices, it will enhance your decision-making in clear and consistent ways. This exercise can help you answer both big-picture and practical questions of life by providing clear vision of what you want your life to ultimately be about.

WATCH HOW YOUR CLEARLY DEFINED OBJECTIVES IN A SPECIFIC RELATIONSHIP HELP YOU CHOOSE DIFFERENTLY.

Briefly look at the answers I shared above about what I want my wife to say about me at the end of my life. If I read my heartfelt answers early in my day, do you think it might have a positive impact on my decisions related to my wife throughout that day? Can you see how my vision as a husband might be clearer that day?

If you want to personally experience how the Rocking Chair exercise is valuable, take this challenge. As you make your way through this book, *read through your answers to this exercise once each day.* Watch how your clearly defined objectives in a specific relationship help you choose differently.

Because this exercise has so much potential value, it is best to view your answers as a working document. It is something that you can add to and fine-tune for the rest of your life. We will revisit your answers to the questions above later in this book and give you a chance to read thoughtful answers from others to the same questions—answers you may find encouraging, challenging, and valuable.

Using the rocking chair exercise is like looking through a telescope. It allows you to see the destination you are aiming for, long before you arrive. Let's take a closer look at the journey to our intended destination. How will we get there? ∎

CHAPTER ONE REVIEW & SMALL GROUP QUESTIONS

1. At what point have you had the clearest vision for what you will care about most at the end of your life?

_____

_____

_____

_____

_____

_____

2. When you think of "your joy and crown" at the culmination of your life, what are you most tempted to put before people?

_____

_____

_____

_____

_____

_____

3. Remember the example of the intentional living of the professional football player. When have you experienced that kind of intentional living? How did that feel?

_____

_____

_____

_____

_____

_____

4. When have you witnessed a painful, nearsighted decision like the one described in the girl's letter to her Dad?

_____

_____

_____

_____

_____

_____

_____

5. Sharing your Rocking Chair responses with others can deepen your relationship with them and help clarify the vision of others for their own life. Consider sharing some of your answers with your family, a close friend, or your small group.

_____

_____

_____

_____

_____

_____

_____

CHAPTER TWO

THE LESSON OF
THE COMPASS

You can't do anything about the length of your life but you can do something about its width and depth.

— Henry Louis Mencken

In the first millennium after Christ, Greeks discovered that the earth was one very large magnet. By the 11th century, the Chinese had invented the compass. Navigation has never been the same.

In the last twenty years, the Global Positioning System, or GPS, has replaced the compass in many applications, but it has not made the compass obsolete.

If you purchase a brand new forty million dollar business jet today, do you know what it will have on board to navigate? Of course it will have the latest and greatest dual GPS navigation system with all the bells and whistles, but it will also still have a compass. When the on-board computers decide not to cooperate or when there is a major electrical failure, the GPS cannot come to your aid. However, the compass is still there, ready to help you find a safe spot to land.

NAVIGATION IS LIFE OR DEATH

The reason you still find a compass on every airplane and every ship is because navigation is important. In fact, many sailors, aviators, and explorers would say navigation is "life or death."

In 1914, Earnest Shackleton led an expedition of twenty-eight men, hoping to be the first to cross the continent of Antarctica. Unexpected ice flows well short of the South Pole halted their progress, trapped their ship, and then slowly but surely crushed their vessel. Shackleton and his men began an epic journey across hundreds of miles of ice and frigid waters in an attempt to survive.

Fifteen months after leaving his ship, Shackleton and his men had made it to Elephant Island and were waiting for rescue. The men were living under lifeboats, eating and burning seal blubber to stay alive, and coming to grips with the fact that no search party was coming.

Six men set out in a twenty-two-foot lifeboat to cross 800 miles of rough and icy waters in hopes of finding help to save the entire crew. The lives of twenty-eight men rested on the guidance of one compass in the hands of one navigator.

Sixteen days after what many of them thought was a final goodbye to their crewmates, the lifeboat arrived at South Georgia Island. One week later, a haggard Earnest Shackleton stumbled into a remote Norwegian whaling camp, and his entire crew was eventually saved. [1]

The Bible also tells us that navigation is of life or death importance. When Jesus spoke of a wide road and a narrow road, each led to a different destination: one described as destruction, or eternal death, and the other eternal life. Taking the right path to the right destination could not be of greater significance.

If we believe this to be true, how do we get to the right destination?

ANSWERING THE QUESTION—WHERE?

If you are going on a journey, you must first choose the destination. Once you set the destination, you can map out the route or course you will take. After you know the course, you can determine the direction and compass heading. You are then ready to set out with reasonable hope of arriving where you have planned.

It is crucial for us to realize that meaningful navigation hinges on the selection of the destination. Even the greatest means of transportation with the best navigational system in the world is not much help on a journey unless you know the destination.

Most of us would never begin a journey without a destination in mind. Yet, all of us at times take steps forward—or make decisions—in our lives without a clear idea of where we are heading.

> IF YOU ARE GOING ON A JOURNEY, YOU MUST FIRST CHOOSE THE DESTINATION.

Some of us have a vague notion of what we are aiming for and declare we are aiming for "happiness" or "financial security" or "a good life for my family" or even "heaven." But in reality, we do not have clear vision for where we are going. An honest evaluation of our choices inevitably reveals that lack of vision.

Your destination is the desired picture of the sum of your life at the end. It is the reality of what you have lived for and what your life has brought about. It is like the finish line of a race that is one step away from our ultimate destination, heaven or hell (or wherever you believe your soul will be in eternity).

Our understanding of the afterlife, while important, contains many facets that will be unclear until we arrive. Considering our destination at the end of our lives allows us to work with entirely understood elements, which casts a clearer vision.

If you're wondering *how precisely* do you need to determine the destination for your journey, the answer is, *the more clarity of vision the better.*

People from all over the United States vacation in Colorado—and for good reason. The scenery in much of Colorado is breathtaking. But when these travelers select Colorado as their vacation destination, they do not jump online looking for lodging and select: "Anywhere in Colorado."

Such an approach might result in spending their vacation in eastern Colorado, which is filled with fine people, but none of the mountain majesty Colorado is known for. Wise vacation planners look closely at the maps, pictures, and reviews so they can be as precise as possible in selecting their destination. We should aim to do the same with our lives.

Consider the difference between these two statements:

1. "When I'm gone, I hope my kids say I was a good mom."

2. "At the end of my life, my children will say, 'My mom showed her love by spending time with me.' "

You could replace "mom" with "dad" in both statements. The first statement is vague and provides little practical guidance for the decisions you might make related to your children. In contrast, the second statement provides a vivid theme to guide your choices.

Clarifying your destination can make a tremendous difference in your life. It can help pave the way so your choices are careful, thoughtful, and intentional, and *not* wasted or foolish. A clearly defined destination is the vision each person needs to determine the right course and stay on that course.

The rocking chair exercise can help you see the destination with precision. We will revisit and provide a chance for you to sharpen your own personal vision for your destination in Chapter Four.

After we have determined our destination, the second crucial step awaits. We must select a compass.

SELECTING YOUR COMPASS

Some people wonder if they have a compass. Everybody has a compass of some sort. Your "compass" is what you use to make choices in your life. Many Christ-followers would say their compass is the Bible, understood with the help of the Holy Spirit. The writers of the canon appear to concur with this understanding. The Psalmist said, *"Your Word is a lamp to my feet and a light for my path."* — Psalm 119:105

YOUR "COMPASS" IS WHAT YOU USE TO MAKE CHOICES IN YOUR LIFE.

The Bible reveals three aspects of God that can guide our choices—His will, His character, and His values.

In His will we have the directives we are to follow out of our love for, and trust in, Him. For example, *"Love your neighbor as yourself."* —Leviticus 19:18 Or, *"Be completely humble and gentle."* —Ephesians 4:2

In His character we understand what He is like and what we should be like as His followers. *"The Lord, the Lord, the compassionate and gracious God."* —Exodus 34:6 As children of God, those made in His image, our choices should be compassionate and gracious.

In His values we see what He cares about and what we should care about. *"For I, the LORD, love justice; I hate robbery and wrongdoing."* —Isaiah 61:8 Our choices should embody justice and conquer unrighteousness.

The will, character, and values of God provide a tried and true instrument with which we can navigate. Sometimes we view the Bible as a compass that can only be trusted part of the time. It is one source of wisdom to consider, but it is not something to be followed in every situation. However, this half-hearted approach, in flying or in life, is filled with danger.

Less than half of the people who become a pilot go on to achieve an instrument rating, the qualification that allows pilots to fly in all kinds of weather. Achieving this level of expertise takes a great deal of study, memorization, and practice.

One of the first fundamentals you learn in instrument flying is the axiom, "Trust your instruments." The importance of this precept is proven in countless stories of pilots who have lost their lives because they failed to believe what their instruments were telling them. Many near tragedies have been averted because pilots who had become disoriented trusted the information displayed on the instruments rather than their feelings.

THE WORD OF GOD IS DESCRIBED AS PERFECT, TRUSTWORTHY, RIGHTEOUS, PURE, AND TRUE.

The Bible echoes this principle. The Word of God is described as perfect, trustworthy, righteous, pure, and true. It is meant to be trusted, even above our feelings. Great things are promised to those who faithfully use the Bible as their compass. The Psalmist said they will live pure lives. Jesus said they will find nourishment and will withstand the storms of life. James said they will be blessed. Peter said they will escape the corruption of the world. Paul said they will be thoroughly equipped for life. [2]

For those who listen to God's Word but do not trust it enough to put it into practice, we find solemn warnings. The Bible tells us these people will not hold up in the storms of life. They are described as deceived. They are said to be fools—like people who look at themselves in the mirror and then immediately forget what they look like. [3]

What will you use to navigate? Determining what you will use as your compass for the journey of life is a supreme decision. Regardless of what you tell *others* is the compass for your life, you may find it eye-opening to reflect on how you make choices and what that tells you about your *actual* compass.

Is your first consideration, when you make choices, the will, character, and values of God found in the Bible? Do you trust the directions He provides? If you are using another primary source of direction, do you consider that more reliable than the Bible? Thinking about these questions is time well-spent. Choose your compass carefully.

CHECKING YOUR COMPASS

Once we have selected our compass, we must learn how to effectively use it to guide us so we stay on course and reach our intended destination. The primary means of remaining on course when flying an airplane is to regularly look at, or check, your compass. * Carefully looking at your compass will tell you when you are on course and when you are off course.

What is the value of each of us learning to check his or her compass? Note that we all will drift off course at some point in our lives. Let me reiterate: *We will all drift off course.* If we need convincing of this, we only need to look at the lives of Abraham, King David, Peter, and plenty of modern-day saints.

Regardless of where you pick your heroes from—whether history (Abraham Lincoln), the sports world (Tim Tebow), those who hold the highest positions of power and influence (President Obama), those with the greatest business acumen (Warren Buffet),

---

* Or the instrument that provides compass and course information together, which is normally the case today.

or even those who have told millions about the love of God (Billy Graham)—every one of them has drifted off course at different points in their journey. We must be ready for this as well.

Checking our compass will prepare us to face our own missteps and the messy seasons of life with hope and a plan to get back on course.

Looking at your compass once an hour when flying will not keep you on course. The compass must be consulted frequently. Good pilots check their compass often enough to notice each time they drift off course. Their goal is to spend as little time drifting and as much time on course as possible.

Our goal should be the same so our lives have the impact they are designed to have. In the second half of this book, we will assist you in developing a tool for you to check your compass carefully and frequently so you have the greatest likelihood of arriving at your intended destination.

> OUR GOAL SHOULD BE THAT OUR LIVES HAVE THE IMPACT THEY ARE DESIGNED TO HAVE.

COURSE CORRECTIONS

When you check your compass and notice you are off course, you make what is called, a course correction. During the Apollo 11 mission to the moon, Mission Control informed Neil Armstrong and the rest of the crew that their instruments and calculations had determined the lunar lander was headed for an orbit above the moon that was too high and would mean failure for the mission.

The only solution was a course correction. Mission Control radioed the details of the correction to the crew. At the precise moment, the crew fired the engines for a specific duration.

Because Mission Control identified the problem in the early stage of the voyage, the course correction required a mere three-second burn of the rocket engines. This seemingly minor adjustment (which took about the same amount of time you spent reading this sentence) changed the spacecraft height above the moon by 115 miles and was the difference between failure and success. [4]

NASA has observed that course corrections are inevitable. Even though the brightest minds and best computers in the world aim their spacecraft toward the intended destination, slight course corrections are necessary on each and every mission.

NASA now schedules specific points in the mission to check the spacecraft's position (their version of checking the compass) and fire the positioning engines so it remains on course. NASA has made course corrections part of its plan.

We have a God who not only allows course corrections but is delighted to help us make them. And in the process, He demonstrates His compassion, mercy, and goodness. Through these course corrections, He proves His ability to guide our lives. He deepens our trust and moves us forward on the important journey of surrendering our control over to Him.

LOCATION VERSUS DESTINATION

As you read this, you probably fall into one of three categories. You may feel like you are right on course with a well-defined destination. Or you might see yourself as generally headed in the right direction but feel you have drifted a bit off course in this season of life. Or maybe you find yourself in a spot that is completely different than you ever wanted and already feel a great deal of regret. In any case, your assessment today is not the end of the story.

Your location is where you are at this point in time. Your destination is where you are headed, where you finish, and ultimately where you will spend the rest of your existence. God has provided His Word, His Spirit, and others who follow Him to help you get on course, stay on course, and see when you are veering off course and headed for the wrong destination. If we will trust in Him and His ways, He will guide us as a shepherd guides his sheep.

> *The LORD is my Shepherd; I have all that I need.*
> *He lets me rest in green meadows;*
> *He leads me beside peaceful streams.*
> *He renews my strength.*
> *He guides me along right paths, bringing honor to His name.*
> *Even when I walk through the darkest valley,*
> *I will not be afraid, for You are close beside me.*
>
> —Psalm 23:1-4 (NLT)

With the Good Shepherd in view, there is great reason for hope. And you have choices to make. ∎

CHAPTER TWO REVIEW & SMALL GROUP QUESTIONS

1. Think of a time when you saw the importance of navigation and having a reliable instrument to help you get to the right destination.

_____

_____

_____

_____

_____

_____

2. What have you been using as your primary instrument(s) to make decisions in your life? On a scale of 1 to 10, how trustworthy is the Bible as a source of direction for life? Why do you believe this?

_____

_____

_____

_____

_____

_____

3. Recall a time where you observed a person you admired drift off course. Who was affected? How did you feel?

_____

_____

_____

_____

_____

_____

4. What course corrections have you made in the past that you are grateful for today?

_____

_____

_____

_____

_____

_____

_____

5. What course corrections have you been contemplating but not yet made? What is holding you back?

_____

_____

_____

_____

_____

_____

_____

CHAPTER THREE

LIFE IS ABOUT CHOICES

Remembering that I'll be dead soon is the most important tool I've ever encountered to help me make the big choices in life. Because almost everything—all external expectations, all pride, all fear of embarrassment or failure—these things just fall away in the face of death, leaving only what is truly important.

— Steve Jobs

What do you do first thing every day when you hear the alarm go off? You either hit snooze or get up. You make a choice. What do you do next? You may roll out of bed to pray, go brush your teeth, make a beeline to the coffee pot, or jump in the shower. You have made another choice.

How do you end the day? Do you spend the last few minutes before you close your eyes reading in bed? Reflecting on the day with your spouse? Staring at the ceiling wondering how you can fix an ailing relationship? Calculating the latest possible time you can set your alarm and still get the kids out the door on time? However you choose to end your day, you end it with a choice.

Our days are made up of choice after choice after choice.

Our choices are enormously important. The choices you make—what you choose to think about, what you choose to say, and what you choose to do—are the most significant thing about you. Your choices, like your fingerprints and your DNA, make you truly unique. No other human will ever have the same thoughts, speak the same words, and do the same things as you. Your character, reputation, and legacy also are made by your choices. While you are here and after you are gone, you will be known by them.

Our choices, more than anything else, impact our moment-by-moment existence. The final accounting of our time on this earth will principally be based on the choices we made.

> OUR CHOICES, MORE THAN ANYTHING ELSE, IMPACT OUR MOMENT-BY-MOMENT EXISTENCE.

Of course we all recognize that not all choices are the same. Which parking space I choose normally has little impact in contrast to the decision of how much time will I spend that day with my spouse or child. Our choices have different levels of importance, but virtually all of them have some identifiable measure of meaning.

Using our navigational metaphor, our choices make up the millions of steps in the journey of our life. Each choice has a direction and a distance. The choices, when linked together, make up our course and determine our destination. Therefore, grasping the role and significance of our choices is the equivalent of learning how to interpret the flight instruments as a pilot. You can attempt to fly an airplane without understanding the cockpit gauges, but it is a scary endeavor that will probably not end well.

CHOICE AND THE IMAGE OF GOD

Part of being made in the image of God is the ability for humans to consider the importance of their choices. No other living thing has this capacity. A dolphin can learn to jump through a hoop for a piece of fish, but it cannot swim around contemplating how its performance during the next show might affect the trainer's self-image.

Humans are uniquely endowed with this capability, and it is not easily removed from us. Viktor Frankl was a Jewish man who spent more than three years in German concentration camps during World War II, including several months at Auschwitz. He wrote:

> *The experiences of camp life show that man does have a choice of action. There were enough examples, often of a heroic nature, which proved that apathy could be overcome, irritability suppressed. Man can preserve a vestige of spiritual freedom [. . .] even in such terrible conditions of psychic and physical distress.*
>
> *We who lived in concentration camps can remember the men who walked through the huts comforting others, giving away their last piece of bread. They may have been few in number, but they offer sufficient proof that everything can be taken from a man but one thing: the last of human freedoms—to choose one's attitude in any given set of circumstances, to choose one's own way.* [1]

Not only are we uniquely given this ability, we are exhorted to recognize and remember the weight of our decisions. This is a core value in the Bible. In the earliest chapters of the Bible (Genesis 2 and 3), God gives Adam and Eve the freedom to choose and then gives them long-lasting consequences because of their choices.

In the final chapters of Scripture (Revelation 20-22), all people are judged and rewarded by eternity with God or eternity without God *based on their choices.* Jesus proclaims, *"Behold, I am coming soon! My reward is with me and I will give to everyone according to what he has done."* —Revelation 22:12

We find a classic example early in the history of God's people. Moses stood before God's people just before they would cross into the Promised Land and said, *"This day... I have set before you life and death, blessings and curses. Now choose life."*—Deuteronomy 30:19

"Life" in this verse means the rich and purposeful existence you find only in loving the Lord and following His ways. "Death" in this verse means the meaningless and destructive life you find in being your own guide or following another god. Moses declares that we make a choice between true life with blessing and the counterfeit life with curses.

Moses goes on to say, *"So that you and your children may live."* He intensifies the situation by stating that our choice between life following God or life on our own will have an undeniable impact on the lives of our children. God must want us to grasp this point because He makes it more than thirty times in the Old Testament.

Ask a sociologist, counselor, or pastor today if the following is true. When someone sits down with a counselor to figure out a problem, it will not take long for the counselor to ask about the "family of origin." The counselor needs to know what life was like in the home when their client was growing up. In essence, the counselor wants to see what choices the father and mother made. This sheds critical light on why the particular person is where he is today.

It is a sobering thought to accept that my choices will have a lasting effect on my children and then on my children's children.

The Bible offers us a clear understanding of the significance of our choices. Yet, it seems all too easy to become blinded to this reality. We can easily find stories that illustrate how bright, successful people fail to see the importance of their decisions.

Several years ago, Tiki Barber, a professional athlete turned TV personality left his pregnant wife and two kids for a college-age network intern. This same man had experienced the sting of his father's adultery and divorce while growing up.

In an interview five years before his own decision to leave his wife for another woman, he spoke about his parent's split and its effects:

> *"I don't give a [expletive] that the relationship didn't work . . .*
> *Not only did he abandon her, I felt like he abandoned us for*
> *a lot of our lives. I have a hard time forgiving that."* [2]

This man who was abandoned as a child chose to abandon his children and his wife, pregnant with twins. The assessment of this man is forever changed by his choices. No one will call him noble, heroic, or selfless. Nobody who knows the truth will name his or her child after him.

There is still hope for this man. With Christ, there is forgiveness, redemption, restoration, and transformation. But we do him, his family, and ourselves no favors by glossing over the harsh effects of what he has done.

His story forces us to ask and answer a key question. *Can we "undo" the choices we make?*

CAN WE "UNDO" THE CHOICES WE MAKE?

We all appreciate the "Undo" function found in almost every software application. As I type this, I can go under the Edit menu and "Undo" the last thing I typed. If I want, I can go back and "Undo" the last fifteen changes I have made to this document.

Unfortunately, life does not have an "Undo" button. If I yell at one of my children, "You are the laziest child I have ever seen," I can ask for forgiveness but I cannot "undo" my choice of words. There can be healing in our relationship but neither of us will ever forget what I said.

DOWNPLAYING WHAT OUR CHOICES MEAN

In this quest to accurately assess the significance of our choices, we must confront a universal trend: Humans are inclined to *minimize* the importance of their choices.

There are exceptions. We know the marriage decision is big and that the choice to have children has long-lasting effects. We see certain athletes or executives over-emphasizing their roles when they have achieved great success. But our tendency is to forget, or consciously underrate, how much our choices mean.

Why might we downplay the impact of our choices? Possibly because we cannot see the difference they make. Perhaps because we are not very proud of the decisions we have made. Maybe we do it because life is passing by so fast that we have little time to reflect on what our choices are bringing about.

The answer may be linked to the fact that we naturally do not like accountability. Simply put, we would prefer to not give an account for what we do. Some have argued this was the seedbed of Darwinian thought and the theory of evolution. If we attribute meaning and impact to human choices, this allows for accountability and judgment. If we remove the meaning and impact from our decisions, we are free from accountability.

Theological concerns have likely contributed toward minimizing the significance of our choices as well. Christianity is distinctive from all other religions in its foundational premise. God revealed Himself to people, God invited them into relationship with Himself, and God came to earth and died on the Cross to make it all possible. GOD DID IT!

We are right to be careful of the mindset of "I did it." Yet, is it biblical to say that our thoughts, words, and actions are not important to God and His Kingdom? I do not believe so. Page after page of the Bible highlights the thoughts, words, and actions of people in relation to God. The Bible reveals God interacting in His righteousness with our choices.

Consider the instances in the Bible where God's people drifted off course: Adam and Eve, Cain, Lot, people in the time of the Judges, David and Bathsheba, Solomon, people in the time of the Exile, the Pharisees, the Corinthians, and the churches in Revelation.

Did they have trouble because they attributed too much importance to their thoughts, words, and actions...or too little? The Bible, rightly read, teaches us to live careful, thoughtful, and intentional lives because our choices *are* important.

> THE BIBLE REVEALS GOD INTERACTING IN HIS RIGHTEOUSNESS WITH OUR CHOICES.

We might fear that emphasizing the importance of our choices will create godless egomaniacs—people who see themselves as the center of the universe and the source of everything good. But could it be that the opposite is true? God is very clear in His Word that He opposes proud people who think they do not need Him and blesses those who humbly recognize their desperate need for Him. Does highlighting the impact of our choices help us see our need for God more or less clearly?

ANOTHER PLAYER

To do justice to this topic, we need to account for another player in the game. The Bible tells us, from start to finish, that we have an enemy known as the Devil. He is a murderer and liar and is continually scheming to steal, kill, and destroy.

It is worth considering that the enemy of our souls wants us to think that our choices are insignificant. What would be the effect on my decisions if Satan could convince me, *it really doesn't matter?*

If I truly believed that, I might have a little more freedom to choose what feels best to me in the moment. If the impact of my choices is negligible, I could make decisions without assessing the impact on my spouse, children, and others. Decisions would be more straightforward since I am the only one to consider.

If I believed my choices made very little difference, I could be carefree with my words instead of choosing them carefully. If I felt anger, I could just let it flow because it felt better to express it than hold it in. I could set my thoughts on whatever was pleasurable to me at the time because my thought life would have no tangible effect on me or anyone else.

> IF I BELIEVED MY CHOICES MADE VERY LITTLE DIFFERENCE, I COULD BE CAREFREE WITH MY WORDS INSTEAD OF CHOOSING THEM CAREFULLY.

Can you see why someone who hates us would want us to believe that our choices did not matter that much? It would allow us to live a thoroughly self-centered life – a life with very little eternal purpose.

Ultimately, what is the result of downplaying the importance of our choices? In the terms of our navigational metaphor, we will find ourselves off course more often and making more choices we will regret.

On the other hand, if I believe my choices are important, making up the path to my destination in life, what will be the effect then?

I had the privilege of assisting the doctor during the delivery of my second child. When the doctor mentioned the idea that I could "catch" our daughter and be the first one to hold her, I thought he was joking. When I responded affirmatively, he promised to be right beside me and tell me everything I needed to do.

When the time came, the physician coached my wife and me through each step. No doubt, I had the easy part. As my beautiful wife labored, my hands became the doctor's instruments. I did exactly what he said, exactly when he said it.

And then, the moment of awe.

I think I stopped breathing as I held my daughter close to my chest and she took her first breath. A flood of emotions washed over me—worship of my God, love for my wife, adoration of this child, and gratitude in being her daddy.

I had not met this doctor before that day, but I listened and followed his instructions with extreme concentration because I knew the potential ramifications of my actions. I was completely dependent on the doctor because I knew what was at stake.

Recognizing that our thoughts, words, and actions are full of meaning and impact can clarify our need for God's minute-by-minute guidance and assistance more than anything else. Understanding the importance of our choices—big and small—can help us check our compass often, trust our instruments, and make choices based on the wisdom of God—choices we will not regret when we one day sit in the rocking chair. ∎

CHAPTER THREE REVIEW & SMALL GROUP QUESTIONS

1. Reread Victor Frankyl's quote in this chapter. On a scale from 1 to 10, how much do you agree that we can choose our attitude and way even in the most difficult set of circumstances?

_____

_____

_____

_____

_____

_____

_____

2. What is the best example you have seen of a father's/mother's choices having a lasting effect on their children? On their children's children?

_____

_____

_____

_____

_____

_____

_____

3. Are there any Biblical examples that come to mind that highlight God's desire for us to understand the importance of our choices?

_____

_____

_____

_____

_____

_____

4. Remember the example of carefully following the doctor's every instruction during the birth of our child. Can you think of a time you were completely dependent on someone else because you knew what was at stake?

_____

_____

_____

_____

_____

_____

_____

5. Do you think highlighting the significance of our choices will make you more or less dependent upon God each day? Why?

_____

_____

_____

_____

_____

_____

_____

CHAPTER FOUR

REVISITING OUR VIEW FROM THE ROCKING CHAIR

If you attempt to talk with a dying man about sports or business, he is no longer interested. He now sees other things as more important. People who are dying recognize what we often forget, that we are standing on the brink of another world.

— William Law

Let's return to the rocking chair perspective. We started with the idea that what we will care about at the end of our lives should be what we care about, and set the stage for, now. Relationships with God, family, and others—and what happens through those relationships—will be at the top of the list of what we will care about as we approach the finish line of our lives

We established that a clearly-defined destination can make a tremendous difference in the direction of your journey. We provided the "Rocking Chair" exercise to help you more precisely define the destination for which you are aiming.

In Chapter Two, we discussed in more detail the navigational metaphor, presenting the selection of a compass and course corrections as necessary steps.

In Chapter Three, we highlighted the role of our choices and why they are so significant. Our daily choices represent the millions of individual steps in the journey of life. When linked together, they make up our course and ultimately determine our destination.

With this review fresh in our minds, we want to provide an opportunity for you to read some thoughtful answers from others to the same questions you answered in the "Rocking Chair" exercise at the end of Chapter One. Our experience has convinced us that we benefit in thinking about these things with others. We've found it very valuable to listen to others as they share their hopes and dreams.

Every time we get to listen to a group of people share their answers to these questions, I hear at least one or two responses that clearly articulate what I hope to be able to say at the end of my life. If any of these answers express your heartfelt desire, we encourage you to add them to your list in Chapter One.

Don't feel like your original answers are competing with these. If you will allow it, these responses can continue to hone your vision for your destination.

THE VIEW FROM THE ROCKING CHAIR

At the end of my life, my spouse will say…

- *He was tenacious in his love for God and for us.*
- *She really loved me, overlooked my faults, and accepted me for who I am.*
- *He laid down his life for me and our family.*
- *She was my helpmate, my biggest cheerleader, and my best friend.*
- *He treated me the same way regardless of who we were with.*
- *She gave me the freedom to become the man God meant me to be.*
- *He always made me feel comfortable sharing my heart.*
- *She loved me faithfully, held nothing back, and honored me in every way.*
- *He challenged me to trust God fully in every situation.*
- *She never complained and she was the best listener.*
- *He always drew me back to God's best for my life.*
- *She lived out her love for God by example—especially to me.*
- *My most joyful moments were spent with him.*

THE VIEW FROM THE ROCKING CHAIR

At the end of my life, my children will say…

- *I've come to trust in the Lord because of the way my dad treated me.*

- *My mom studied the Word with fervency and served our family with joy.*

- *My dad always loved to be with me and listen to me.*

- *She taught me by her words and actions how to love the Lord and be a godly woman.*

- *My dad faithfully taught me God's Word.*

- *Mama listened and she loved and she understood. She was not too busy.*

- *My dad always helped me work out any difficulty I was in without condemnation.*

- *She taught me the importance of daily devotions and quiet time with the Lord.*

- *I was always more important to my dad than anyone outside our family.*

- *She loved and respected my dad and taught me how important that is in my own marriage.*

- *My dad was slow to become angry, and if he did become angry, he was always in control of his words and actions.*

- *He lived his life the way I want to live mine.*

- *She modeled a transparent, vibrant, and authentic relationship with Jesus.*

- *Dad was my guide and trainer for this life.*

THE VIEW FROM THE ROCKING CHAIR

At the end of my life, my friends will say…

- *You showed true interest in me and poured wisdom into my life.*
- *You stuck with me through good times and bad times.*
- *He was truly grateful for everything that God had done in his life.*
- *She made me laugh and I saw the joy of the Lord in her.*
- *You were a steadfast friend no matter what.*
- *She was really transparent. What you saw was what you got.*
- *She loved the Lord above all else.*
- *He increased my appetite for the Lord.*
- *She did not judge me.*
- *You helped me see the Lord's will in every situation.*
- *Your yes was yes, and your no was no.*
- *She made time for me and our friendship was irreplaceable.*
- *No one could come between you and your God, you and your wife, or you and your kids.*
- *You always asked the right questions at the right times, always out of love.*

THE VIEW FROM THE ROCKING CHAIR

At the end of my life, my Lord will say…

- *Well done good and faithful servant.*
- *You trusted Me more than your fear of failure.*
- *Even when things were difficult, you didn't turn aside.*
- *See, I told you so. In My Presence is fullness of joy; at My right hand there are pleasures forevermore!*
- *You surrendered it all to Me and I used you to change lives.*
- *You brought Me glory by the way you loved others.*
- *You trusted Me with everything in your life.*
- *You let Me heal you and others—you were My vessel.*
- *I saw your efforts and your consistency with your eyes on Me.*
- *Well done, good and faithful son! Your children's children follow me with all their hearts!*
- *As I poured into you, you poured into others.*
- *You loved what I loved.*
- *You showcased My gospel with your life.*
- *I love you daughter. Welcome home.*

If you are married, we highly encourage you to ask your spouse to do the same exercise. Then, set aside some special time together (on a date or after the kids go to bed) to share your answers with each other. If you have school-aged children, you may consider sharing your answers with them. If you are unmarried, consider sharing your answers with a good friend over a cup of coffee.

VALUE OF THE ROCKING CHAIR PERSPECTIVE

Now that you have pictured yourself in the rocking chair and contemplated what you desire those closest to you to say about you at the end of your life, you can see the potential clarity this can provide in decisions you face.

For example, if you are facing a career choice, the rocking chair perspective can help. One of my close friends, who was working in an industry that was tumultuous at the time, called with news that he had been contacted by a recruiter for a government job which promised greater job security.

As we discussed the pros and cons of the new opportunity, I asked if the new job would help or hurt the things he will care about most at the end of his life. After a long pause, he acknowledged that the new job would harm his efforts to be the dad and husband God had called him to be. He turned down the job offer and has never had to second-guess that decision.

In our own lives, there are many day-to-day situations where we can make better choices if we remember the rocking chair outlook. Occasionally my wife has a commitment on a weekday so I get a couple of hours with just my two- and four-year-old. I can try to accomplish work tasks while they play in their rooms or watch a movie. Or I can sit in their room and read books and play "Steamroller," where I roll on the carpet like the piece of road construction equipment and they try to jump or crawl over me before becoming part of the new road surface.

Certainly, there are times when I have a pressing commitment, which requires me to work instead of playing with my kids. But in most instances, both are reasonable options. If I reflect on what I hope they will say about me at the end of my life ("My dad loved to be with me"), I can make this a primary factor in the decision.

It does not mean I will choose playing over work every single time. But I can carefully factor in things like how much time I have spent with these two in the last couple of days and how much time I will have with them over the next few days. I can thoughtfully ask, "What should my choice be in light of what I am hoping they will say and believe about their dad?"

BUT THE REALITY IS WE HAVE ONE LIFE TO LIVE—ONE SET OF CHOICES—AND IT WILL BE OUR STORY FOR ALL ETERNITY.

Ultimately, factoring in your answers from the rocking chair exercise will produce superior decisions—decisions you will not regret.

One crucial note: Your decisions with the rocking chair in view will cost you. Playing with your kids instead of working puts you farther behind on your list of tasks. But it is the right cost for the right gain. Making decisions lined up with what you will care about in the rocking chair will help you stay on course and reach your intended destination.

THE HOURGLASS PERSPECTIVE

Possibly the most compelling reason to keep the rocking chair perspective close at hand is this: We only get one shot at this life.

An hourglass is one of the most captivating symbols. It gives us a picture of something that is constant, intangible, and unstoppable.

Each grain of sand passes from the upper to lower chamber, signifying the passage of time. The hourglass captures the truth that our time left on this earth is continually decreasing. While the rocking chair perspective clarifies what matters most, the hourglass makes vivid the value of our time.

WE ALL HAVE AN UNSEEN HOURGLASS REPRESENTING OUR LIFE. ONLY GOD KNOWS HOW MANY GRAINS OF SAND ARE LEFT.

We all have an unseen hourglass representing our life. On the day our life began, the upper chamber was full of countless grains of sand and the lower chamber was empty. As you read these words, there is some sand left in the upper chamber but much is already resting on the bottom. Only God knows how many grains of sand are left.

In everyday life, most of us have difficulty keeping the hourglass in mind. We feel like there will be an unending supply of sand. We have trouble acknowledging our finite allotment of days, words, and heartbeats.

But the reality is we have one life to live—one set of choices—and it will be our story for all eternity. Once this day is past, you cannot get it back. The fifteen minutes that you have spent reading this chapter will never be available to you again.

There are occasions when it is easier to remember I have only one shot at this life. When I have been on mission trips to foreign countries, I have been able to keep the hourglass in view. If I find a gentleman who is willing to talk to me on a bus in India, I know that I have this one opportunity to make a difference because it is extremely unlikely I will ever see him again. I can attempt to share Christ's love and some words that are eternally significant . . . or not.

When I know my time somewhere is short, I realize the cost of missed opportunities. I choose knowing that I will probably never have another chance.

There are seasons when the hourglass is harder to keep in view. You have probably been part of, or witnessed, a scene like this: An older man or woman in a grocery store checkout line notices a young mom or dad struggling mightily to keep their children contained as the kids reach for candy and ask why they can't have some.

The older man or woman, with children long since moved out of the house, cannot help but say, *"They grow up so fast. Enjoy this time with them. They'll be gone before you know it."*

Why does the older man or woman feel compelled to share this unsolicited council even with perfect strangers? Because they can see now what they could not see when they were in the throes of parenting—the time raising your children is not limitless. It is precious. They want the parents to see the sand is falling.

What is the impact when we cannot remember the truth in the hourglass? When I think I have unlimited time, it makes choosing well less important. I tend to get sloppy in my decision-making. I am more likely to think unfruitful thoughts, say insensitive things, and waste time. There is a sense that I can get things fixed up and finely tuned later. I do not have to be focused on getting it right and staying on course this time if there is always a next time.

What if the one who comes to "steal, kill, and destroy" is the source of the lie that there will always be a next time? What if this

WE CAN WISELY INVEST OUR TIME IN THE THINGS THAT WILL MATTER MOST AT THE END OF OUR LIVES—OR WE CAN "GET AROUND TO THAT LATER."

is part of a plan to keep us from ever getting around to the things that matter most? Our enemy would love to keep us from seeing the reality of the hourglass until it is too late.

Psalm 139:16 declares: *"All the days ordained for me were written in your book before one of them came to be."* God has given us a set number of days to live. We have one set of opportunities and choices. Some have passed us by and some are still before us. How will you invest the time you have been given?

Paul exhorts us: *"Be careful how you live. Don't live like fools, but like those who are wise. Make the most of every opportunity in these evil days. Don't act thoughtlessly, but understand what the Lord wants you to do."* —Ephesians 5:15-17, NLT

We can wisely invest our time in the things that will matter most at the end of our lives—or we can "get around to that later."

But be warned: Later may never come.

It is not only the sand in our own hourglass that we care about. Many years ago, I received a startling phone call from the commander of my flying squadron about two of my friends and fellow pilots. Through a broken voice he said, "We lost Rick and Jim [not their real names] tonight in an airplane crash."

He instructed me to secure all the training records related to these pilots as these materials would be key information in the accident investigation. After my mind finally wrapped around what was happening, my thoughts zeroed in on these questions: *How did I treat each of them? Did I share about my faith with each one? Did I show them the love of God?*

We have friends who lost their twenty-year-old daughter in a tragic car accident. Consider the moment her parents heard the news of the crash and their loss. After the first immense wave of grief, what do you think went through their minds? What would you or I think about in the same situation?

Did we make the most of the time we had with our child? Did we teach and show her about the Lord and His love?

The truth is, we never know when these phone calls will come. We do not know how much sand is left in the hourglass. Whenever the sand runs out—for us or for a loved one or friend—our chance is gone. We do not get another opportunity.

Grappling with this truth is sobering. But if we keep it in mind, it can be a tremendous motivator to live so we will not have significant regrets. The rocking chair perspective and exercise are intended to provide vision and practical goals so you know you have invested well when the last grain of sand has fallen. ▪

CHAPTER FOUR REVIEW&
SMALL GROUP QUESTIONS

1. What were your favorite answers from the Rocking Chair exercises shared by others? Did you add any of these to your own exercise?

_____

_____

_____

_____

_____

_____

2. When has clear long-term vision for your life helped you make a challenging decision? Think of a specific experience.

_____

_____

_____

_____

_____

_____

3. How do you feel when you get to the end of a day in which you have made many choices based on what will matter most at the end of your life?

_____

_____

_____

_____

_____

_____

4. In what aspects of your life can you relate to the common phenomenon of feeling there will be an unlimited number of opportunities?

_____

_____

_____

_____

_____

_____

5. Has there been a time when you have been forced to remember the truth of the hourglass? How has this affected your life?

_____

_____

_____

_____

_____

_____

CHAPTER FIVE

QUESTIONS

My question—that which at the age of fifty brought me to the verge of suicide—was the simplest of questions, lying in the soul of every man . . . a question without an answer to which one cannot live.

It was: What will come of what I am doing today or tomorrow? What will come of my whole life? Why should I live, why wish for anything, or do anything? Is there any meaning in my life that the inevitable death awaiting me does not destroy?

— Leo Tolstoy, *A Confession*

Imagine you are at the emergency room and have just been called back to a treatment room. The nurse bombards you with questions. "How old are you? Do you smoke? Are you on any medications?" If you arrive at the emergency room incapacitated, the staff will follow a set protocol of tests, medical history reviews, and phone calls to family members to get answers to key questions.

In the emergency room, the right question at the right time can mean the difference between life and death. Questions are crucial in the medical profession because they help the doctor discover what is, and is not, functioning correctly.

Similarly, in the courtroom, judges and attorneys alike use questions much like a surgeon uses a scalpel—attempting to uncover critical information—to render a judgment in light of the law. The right question at the right time can bring an end to a trial or seal the fate of an accused. The best attorneys spend countless hours determining the questions they will ask in a deposition or trial because they know the power of good questions.

Doctors and attorneys are not the only ones who place a high value on questions. Teachers, social workers, counselors, leadership consultants, pastors, and, of course, parents, see questions as indispensible.

Why?

Good questions provide a chance to see where you are and where you want to go. Good questions can help you check your compass. Let's continue the discussion about questions.

THE VALUE OF QUESTIONS

When someone comes to you with a declaration about life, you have the option to engage his or her statement or dismiss it. When someone comes to you with a question about life, you are far more likely to thoughtfully consider, respond, and have valuable communication with the questioner. In many situations, a question trumps a declaration in effective communication, especially if relationship is a high value.

Relationships require interaction. Without it, they will decay and eventually they may die. Questions create this interaction. They provide the opportunity for two people to share about themselves and for the relationship to grow.

I can play Legos® alongside my five-year-old son for half an hour and there can be little noise except for the guttural sounds he makes simulating the sound of the car or airplane we have built. But if I choose to ask questions while we play—"Zeke, would you rather ride in a race car or a jet airplane?"—I can learn little facts about my son (he'd rather ride in a race car), and sometimes some not so little facts (loud noises hurt his ears and really scare him). Do you see how our relationship can grow through questions?

When someone asks you a question about your own life, it forces you to introspect. In that introspection, you reflect on your values and behaviors and formulate an answer. Questions allow us to clarify what we believe and to know ourselves better.

In my first semester of seminary, an older, distinguished professor captured the attention of every student in the class with this question, "Do you want to hear the one thing you must know so you will not fail in ministry?"

We were all ears.

He continued, "You will never fail in ministry because you do not know enough Greek. You will not fail in ministry because you cannot exegete [explain] a passage of Scripture. You *will fail* in ministry if you do not know yourself."

It was a shocking statement for a seminary student to hear but one that has helped me appreciate the significance of questions that make me look inward and see the true condition of my heart.

THE POWER OF QUESTIONS

Questions can be a powerful tool to change things. The right questions at the right time can make all the difference in the world to your view from the rocking chair.

Consider this statement from earlier in the chapter: "Relationships require interaction. Without it, they will decay and may eventually die."

Contrast those two declarative sentences with this question, "What happens to relationships when there is no interaction?" If the responder comes to the correct conclusion, he or she is much more likely to remember and place value on that truth. The person who answers may even evaluate his relationships in light of this truth and consider changing the way he acts. There is a greater possibility of transformation when we use questions.

Questions also make a big difference in helping us with "blind spots." Blind spots are harmful attitudes or actions in our lives that we cannot or choose not to see. If someone approaches us attempting to open our eyes to a blind spot with a declarative statement, such as, "In our meeting, your words were offensive," what is the likely reaction?

As Captain Kirk used to say on the original *Star Trek,* "Shields!" We normally get defensive, putting our focus not on the content of what was shared but on the emotion we are feeling. Our next step also follows *Star Trek* protocol: fight or flight. The result usually is not pretty or productive.

Contrast this with someone approaching us with a question, "When you mentioned his background in our meeting, can you see how he may have felt uncomfortable?"

The right question regarding one of our blind spots can help us hear and understand what others see that we may not.

QUESTIONS LEAD US TO CONSIDER THE VALUE OF WHAT IS BEING SHARED.

Questions lead us to consider the value of what is being shared instead of rejecting the statement altogether. If we look inward and honestly review our actions and motives, it may result in the elimination of a blind spot. We may not stumble again in that same way because someone approached us with a thoughtful question.

Questions can help us clarify our direction. With the frenetic pace of life today, many people confess to a decision-making approach that can have a frightful price, "Ready, fire...aim."

When a hunter uses this approach, the cost is no meat in the freezer or paying a fine for shooting an elk instead of a deer. When a soldier uses this approach, the cost can be the failure of a mission or someone dying from friendly fire.

When we use this approach—saying "yes" and "no" to invitations and opportunities without careful evaluation—the cost at first seems much less immediate and dramatic. The cost can be the slow deterioration of relationships we care about or a seeming purposelessness in life. In time, the cost can be the death of a marriage or the reality of a family who knows about God but lives for things that do not really matter.

If we ask questions at the right time about the right things, it can help us put our priorities in order, "Ready, aim…fire." Questions can help us aim carefully and choose well.

JESUS AND QUESTIONS

Jesus asked a lot of questions. Here are some of them:

- *Who do you say I am?* (Matthew 16)
- *What good will it be for a man if he gains the whole world yet forfeits his soul?* (Matthew 16)
- *Why do you look at the speck of sawdust in your brother's eye and pay no attention to the plank in your own eye?* (Matthew 7)
- *Which of you, if his son asks for bread, will give him a stone?* (Matthew 7)
- *You of little faith, why are you so afraid?* (Matthew 8)
- *Do you believe that I am able to do this?* (Matthew 9)

- *Who is my mother and who are my brothers?* (Matthew 12)

- *If a man owns a hundred sheep . . . will he not leave the 99?* (Matthew 18)

- *Can you drink the cup I am going to drink?* (Matthew 20)

- *Am I leading a rebellion that you come out with swords and clubs to capture me?* (Matthew 26)

In the gospel of Matthew alone, Jesus asked eighty-two questions! Why did Jesus ask these questions? Since He was the greatest Teacher ever, we could argue He asked these questions because of their educational value.

Many of the most rigorous training programs utilize questions extensively. Clearly, Jesus was aiming for a transformational learning experience so questions fit the bill.

But the answer goes deeper still. Jesus left heaven to live among us and die for us out of His unfathomable love. Here is a biblical definition for His love: *sacrificially doing what is best for others in light of their needs.*

Why did Jesus ask all these questions even though He knew all the answers? He asked the questions because it was the very best thing for each person in light of their needs.

ALL HIS QUESTIONS FLOWED FROM THE SAME SPRING—PERFECT LOVE.

The questions helped them to see what they needed to see, wrestle with what they needed to wrestle with, remember what they needed to remember, and embrace what they needed to embrace. All His questions flowed from the same spring—perfect love.

OUR USE OF QUESTIONS

In this book, we hope to do what Jesus did. We intend to ask three questions that we think have an extremely important connection to what you will say when you reach the rocking chair.

I believe these are three of the most valuable questions a Christ-follower can ask. I hope as you ask these questions, each one helps you check your compass. We pray that the direction you are currently heading and the direction you want to head both become very clear.

Perhaps the questions will allow you to see what it means to be on course and will also help you to know if the Lord wants you to make any course corrections. Ultimately, we pray these questions help you get to the rocking chair having lived for the most important things.

THE COMPASS CHECK

As you contemplate these questions, we will help you develop a personalized tool called the "Compass Check." The Compass Check, as its name implies, is a set of questions you will develop to help you check your compass for the rest of your days.

Answering these questions will help you see if you are on course and assist you in remaining on course day by day. You will create these questions in light of your answers to the rocking chair exercise and the ideas we will discuss throughout the rest of this book.

There are two types of Compass Check questions—check-up and filter questions.

Check-Up Questions help you evaluate if you are on course and headed for the right destination or not. Consider this example: In the last week, have we played, laughed, and learned about God with our kids?

If I honestly answer "no" to this question, I know I have drifted off course from where I want to be. I have a chance to discover why this has happened with my wife and make the necessary course corrections.

Filter Questions help you carefully and thoughtfully consider new opportunities and requests in light of what you want to be able to say in the rocking chair. One of our family compass check filter questions is: *Would saying "yes" to this commitment fragment our family or bring us together?*

If I can see that an opportunity will likely fragment our family, it is probably best for me to turn it down unless there are exceptional circumstances. It is best to include both "check-up" and "filter" questions on your Compass Check.

Checking your compass regularly is essential if you want to stay on course and reach your desired destination. The Compass Check is a tool you will use daily or weekly. Keep this frequency in mind as you create it. We'll discuss more about how to utilize the Compass Check in the last chapter of this book.

The goal to keep in mind is reminding yourself of the key biblical truths and your desired destination as you make choices through the day.

DEVELOPING YOUR COMPASS CHECK

Once you have finished thinking through each question we present in the following chapters, we will give you a chance to brainstorm potential Compass Check questions.

Then, in the final chapter of this book, we will give you a chance to look at questions other families have found helpful and finalize your personal Compass Check.

We believe the set of questions you develop to check your compass will be valuable and trust the Lord will use it to keep you on course all the way to your destination. ▪

CHAPTER FIVE REVIEW & SMALL GROUP QUESTIONS

1. In what settings have you observed questions being used most effectively?

_____

_____

_____

_____

_____

_____

_____

2. With your children (if applicable) or others you are leading, when have you observed the power of a question?

_____

_____

_____

_____

_____

_____

3. If making a declaration is more expedient than asking questions, when is it worth the extra time and energy to use questions?

_____

_____

_____

_____

_____

_____

4. Do you have a favorite question that God or one of the writers of Scripture asks in the Bible? Why do you like it?

_____

_____

_____

_____

_____

_____

_____

5. What is the best question you have ever been asked? Why was it valuable to you?

_____

_____

_____

_____

_____

_____

_____

CHAPTER SIX

ARE WE AIMING FOR BUSY OR FULL?

The thief comes only to steal, and kill, and destroy. I came that they might have life and have it to the full.

— Jesus

If you walk up to someone in the United States and ask him, "How's life?" What is the answer you expect to hear? If he doesn't give the customary response "good," you will most likely get the answer "busy," or some synonym.

Busyness is an American pandemic. Some would say busyness is an American *addiction*. Nine out of ten families who come to our ranch on retreat are in a full-blown wrestling match with their pace of life.

Here are some remarkable statistics on American families over the last 40 years:

- The average workweek has increased from 41 to 47 hours.

- The number of families that say they regularly dine together has decreased by 33 percent.

- Free time for families has dropped 37 percent.

Ironically, testimony before a Senate subcommittee in 1967 claimed that by 1985 people could be working just twenty-two hours a week or twenty-seven weeks a year due to the efficiencies that technology would bring. [1]

BUSY OR FULL

With this information in mind, let us consider the first question that will help us check our compasses: *Am I aiming for busy or am I aiming for full?*

Here's how we would define the terms:

Busy—hurrying from one thing to the next; feeling like you are behind; easily distracted by future tasks.
Full—sufficient time allotted for each activity; feeling like you are on pace; able to be "present."

THE THREAT OF BUSY

Gordon MacDonald has observed the spiritual landscape of our country for the past forty years. He has served as a pastor, seminary professor and president, and written several books on the inner life. He makes an intriguing statement:

> *"I'm of the opinion that busyness is a deeper threat to the soul than pornography ever was."* [2]

Pornography has had a devastating effect on our society, ripping apart countless marriages and families. After acknowledging that fact, reflect on MacDonald's statement for a few moments. How and why might what he says be true? One thing can be a greater threat than another if we recognize the danger in one and cannot see the danger in another.

Pornography is a known evil. When individuals spend time viewing pornographic images, they recognize a risk to their relationships and to their thought life. In dramatic contrast, busyness is a badge of honor. When we tell someone, directly or indirectly, that we are busy, it provides a sense of self-worth.

In a world where many of us struggle with insecurity, our busyness tells us, "I am needed in so many areas. I must be valuable."

The people we admire, from CEOs to pastors to sports figures, all appear to be living the busy life. We feel that busyness equals productivity, which equals success, wealth, and honor.

How can busyness be dangerous to us? What can it steal from our lives? In order to answer this question, we'd like you to do the following "Busy vs. Full" exercise. It will take fifteen minutes and we think it can change what people will say about you in the rocking chair. Bottom line—doing this exercise is worth it.

First, find a place with few distractions. Second, review the definitions of "busy" and "full." Third, contrast the feelings you have when living the busy life to the feelings you experience living the full life. Record your thoughts. For example:

Busy	Full
Overwhelmed	Peaceful
Frantic	Fruitful

Finally, consider the impact of the busy life versus the full life on some of your relationships. Describe what these relationships are like when living busy and when living full.

Record your thoughts on the following page. For example:

Relationship with God

Checking the box   Interactive fellowship

Relationship with spouse

Communicating "data points"   Sharing thoughts and dreams

Try to list three or four descriptions under each section.

BUSY   FULL

I feel . . .

_____   _____
_____   _____
_____   _____
_____   _____

Relationship with God

_____   _____
_____   _____
_____   _____

Relationship with spouse

_____   _____
_____   _____
_____   _____

Relationship with kids

_____   _____
_____   _____
_____   _____

Relationship with others

_____   _____
_____   _____
_____   _____

This page is also available to print at www.sonrisemountainranch.org/exercises/busy_vs_full.

Here is the exercise with common responses from people who live across the country:

BUSY   # FULL

I feel . . .

BUSY	FULL
Overwhelmed	Peaceful
Frantic	Fruitful
Chaos	Content
Distracted	Fully present
Going through the motions	Purposeful
Resentful	Joyful
Overcommitted	Involved
Exhausted	A "good" tired

Relationship with God

BUSY	FULL
Checking the box	Interactive fellowship
Non-existent	Meaningful
Selfish prayers	Praise & thanksgiving
Shallow	Listening

Relationship with spouse

BUSY	FULL
Business partners	Intimacy
Ships passing in the night	Oneness
Communicating "data points"	Sharing hopes and dreams
Critical	Laughing

Relationship with kids

BUSY	FULL
Yelling at them	Expressing affection
Fixing their behavior	Training their hearts
Rushing them	Playing together
Annoyed	Relishing

Relationship with others

BUSY	FULL
Just one more thing I have to do	Doing life together
Another opportunity for guilt	Rich encouragement

Review your answers one more time from top to bottom. This exercise is an eye-opening experience for most people. Through it, we can see what the busy life steals from us and what the full life brings to us. We can understand that the pace we choose makes a tremendous difference in what life feels like each day. We can grasp how our pace dramatically affects all the relationships we will care about in the rocking chair.

Let's continue our investigation of how wide is the divide between the busy life and the full life.

FIVE SIGNIFICANT CONTRASTS

During past discussions of "Busy vs. Full", many people have found these five contrasts especially valuable.

EMPTY VS. CONTENT

Contentment is something that is highly sought after and yet extremely elusive in our society. People regularly share that the busy life is "empty" and "unsatisfying," while using words such as "content" and "satisfied" to describe the full life. How are pace of life and level of contentment related?

Being overcommitted tends to harm our appreciation of every facet of life so our discontentment grows. Because we feel empty, we say "yes" to too many things, hoping one or all of them will increase our contentment. You see how a vicious cycle can develop.

Conversely, living the "full" life produces a total appreciation for each aspect of life and thus greater contentment. Because we are satisfied, we are careful with our commitments so we can perpetuate, rather than disturb, the current pace. You see how a desirable cycle can be sustained.

GOING THROUGH THE MOTIONS VS. FULLY PRESENT

Maybe you have experienced the difference in busy versus full when reading a book to a child. When I sit down to read a book with my two-year-old daughter while in busy mode, I keep thinking about my to-do list. The clock is ticking in my head. I consider skipping the next four pages and wonder if she will notice.

Why am I reading this book to her even though I am not engaged? I am going through the motions, mostly absent from my daughter, because this is what a "good dad" is supposed to do. I am reading the book for my self-image as a father.

When I sit down to read with my daughter while in full mode, I am with her in the story. I take my time on each page. I watch and enjoy her facial expressions. We laugh together. I answer her question, then another, then another. Why am I reading this book to her? Because our relationship is priceless. I love being with her. Being fully present with someone is one of the greatest gifts you can give—it is an incomparable way of saying "I love you."

LIFE-SUCKING VS. LIFE-GIVING

What is the difference between the two examples above? When I read to my daughter in a hurry, without being engaged, it sucks the life out of me. I know what I am forfeiting and I do it anyway. When I read to my daughter being fully engaged, enjoying the moments, we are sharing life with one another. This is one example among many in our relationships within our families. The difference between busy versus full is clear: life-sucking or life-giving.

DECEPTION VS. INTEGRITY

I've noticed something. When I am living the busy life, I am more often late to meetings.

Imagine that I leave my office for a meeting in town ten minutes later than necessary, because I was trying to accomplish "one more thing" before I left. On my way to town, I find myself behind a farmer on his tractor and it takes a couple of minutes before he lets me pass. I am now twelve minutes late. I speed a little on the way and show up to the meeting, with several men I respect, nine minutes late.

What am I tempted to say as I walk into the room?

"Sorry I'm late. I got stuck behind a tractor on Big Cimarron road."

What have I just done? *Deceived.* The tractor did not make me late—my choices did. Even though my deception will go unnoticed by my friends, I have followed the way of Satan and there is a cost in my life.

The more I live the busy life, the more temptations there are to deceive in the subtlest of ways. Little by little, this acceptance of deception will cause me to drift off course. When I live the full life, I can hold to my word and follow through on my commitments. I can remain on guard against any level of deception and live with the joy and richness that comes with integrity.

CRITICAL VS. GRATEFUL

Think about your relationships. Are you more likely to have a critical spirit toward your spouse if you are living busy or full? Do you express gratitude to God more often when you are praying busy or praying full?

In our relationship with God and others, there seems to be a link between the busy life and critical thoughts. At the same time, the full life and a heart of gratitude seem to also go hand in hand. When the pressure of the busy life comes, we may take some of the blame, but most of us look to others to at least share in it—if not own it outright.

Gratitude normally comes from remembering the goodness, in character or actions, of someone else. Remembering takes time and mental space. So it is not surprising to see a connection between the full life and a grateful heart.

Along with the five contrasts we have just considered, there are also two familiar phrases busy people use that may threaten the arrival to their desired destinations.

"QUALITY TIME VERSUS QUANTITY TIME"

In the last thirty years, countless articles and books have spotlighted the difference between quality and quantity time. Quality time—or time fully engaged doing meaningful things with people—has been advocated over quantity time, an approach that says "more is better" in terms of time together.

The creation of the term "quality time" is beneficial in that it highlights the point that all time spent together is not equal in terms of relational value. Looking into your spouse's eyes over a romantic dinner as you share your dreams with each other is relationally superior to wordlessly sitting next to each other on the couch watching TV. However, the distinction between quality and quantity time may cunningly lead us to accept and even perpetuate the busy life.

A recent study on parent-child communication found that parents and children spend 14.5 minutes per day talking to each other and only two minutes each day in meaningful communication.[3]

If we ultimately believe that relationships with our loved ones do not need large amounts of time to develop but rather small bits of focused time, we have a logical reason to minimize time spent with our spouse and children.

In the face of unending requests and demands for our time, we are stripped of the compelling resolve necessary to make the disciplined choices that bring the full life. Effectively, we will tolerate devoting most of our time and energy to things we will not care about in the rocking chair.

> IF WE ULTIMATELY BELIEVE THAT RELATIONSHIPS WITH OUR LOVED ONES DO NOT NEED LARGE AMOUNTS OF TIME TO DEVELOP . . . WE HAVE A LOGICAL REASON TO MINIMIZE TIME SPENT WITH OUR SPOUSE AND CHILDREN.

"IT'S ONLY A SEASON"

Since we have had children, there have been a number of times where my short-term evaluation of how much time I had been devoting to my family was dismal. Ironically, one of the most challenging seasons was when we were beginning renovations on a property that would serve as a family retreat center to help families invest their time in eternally significant things.

My wife and I were both wearing what seemed to be five different hats and trying to care for our four young children. Between the preparations, visitors, volunteers, and unexpected water outages, it felt like we needed at least a thirty-six-hour day to keep up.

Two weeks after we began renovations, we experienced a little family meltdown with tears, raised voices, and a general feeling of bewilderment. As I reflected on how we had gotten there, it was obvious that I had been giving almost all of my time to the project. I argued it out in my mind: *It is just a season and it will not last forever.*

My wife and I have heard those words from so many couples on retreat as they reflect on the busyness of their lives. While the statement, "It's only a season" may be valid, it presumes we know what the future holds. What if the demands in the next season of life are the same or greater than this one?

For so many families, this "season" is followed by another that is equally challenging in terms of the demands for their time. What if the current season lasts much longer than expected? Many couples find themselves admitting the current season that they thought would last three months has actually lasted two years. And as they look ahead, there is no good reason to think things will change.

> WHAT IF THE DEMANDS IN THE NEXT SEASON OF LIFE ARE THE SAME OR GREATER THAN THIS ONE?

Many of us are "time optimists." We have this sense that our schedules will let up and we will be able to spend time on the things that really matter once we reach a specific point a little farther down the road.

But what if that point out in front of us is really like the mirage of an oasis in the desert? We are parched and desperately in need of cool refreshment and see that place up ahead where we can finally have life-giving water. But as we plod ahead together as a family, the oasis does not get any closer. We find ourselves left with little strength for what we really need—a change in our direction and perspective.

"It's only a season."

If you use this phrase or identify with this kind of thinking, make sure you do not allow it to become an excuse to neglect those whose opinions will matter most in the rocking chair. Be on guard that this phrase does not become a justification for forgoing course corrections regarding the way you spend your time.

Take a moment and reflect if you have ever been caught in either of these time traps. Resolve to walk the rest of the journey with a realistic view of both. Commit to helping others not fall into these traps.

. . . .

Carefully considering this question of busy versus full requires a "no sugarcoating" policy.

In *Good to Great*, business leadership author Jim Collins writes, "You cannot make a series of good decisions without first confronting the brutal facts!" [4] So now let us confront the brutal facts about the busy life. If we persist in the busy life, what might it cost us? ▪

CHAPTER SIX REVIEW & SMALL GROUP QUESTIONS

1. Which comparisons from the Busy vs. Full exercise were most significant to you? Why?

_____

_____

_____

_____

_____

_____

_____

2. Which one of your relationships do you think has been most affected by busyness in the last year? What happened?

_____

_____

_____

_____

_____

_____

_____

3. Of the five contrasts we considered, which one provides the greatest motivation to live the full life?

_____

_____

_____

_____

_____

_____

_____

4. We discussed how the phrases "Quality versus quantity time" and "It's only a season" can create traps. When have you seen this happen in your own life?

_____

_____

_____

_____

_____

_____

5. After reading this chapter, how would you describe the threat of busyness?

_____

_____

_____

_____

_____

_____

CHAPTER SEVEN

THE COST OF
THE BUSY LIFE

*The most winsome people in the world are the people who make
you feel that they are never in a hurry.*

— F. W. Boreham

As we discussed in the last chapter, we are prone to look at busyness as a positive thing in our lives. In fact, many of us may treat busyness like a pet Golden Retriever. We spend time with Busyness. We pet and hug Busyness. We feed and take Busyness for a walk. When friends come over, we show Busyness off to our friends. We teach our children to play with Busyness and feel most comfortable when Busyness is curled up close by.

What if the reality is that "Busyness" is not a Golden Retriever but instead a full-grown king cobra?

The one who first appeared in the garden as a serpent has hatched an insidious scheme in our day "to steal, kill, and destroy." Using his signature style of deception and masquerading one thing for another, Satan has convinced most of us that Busyness is our friendly family pet, not an aggressive, agile, killer.

You would never let a wild cobra live in your house and around your family. Why? Because you would know it was just a matter of time before one of your loved ones would be hurt or killed by the cobra.

If you had a cobra in your house, what would you do? You would get a machete, gun, or club of some sort and you would KILL IT. If it did not die right away, you would continue hacking, shooting, or beating it until you were sure it was dead.

Since busyness is so deeply rooted in our society, we will only treat busyness like a cobra if we clearly comprehend what it could cost us.

Bill Hybels, pastor of Willow Creek Church in Chicago, received a letter from a man who didn't understand the cost of the busy life during the height of his career:

Let me state my position on the matter of your needing to slow down. I think I have a better-than-average perspective based on my past experience of ten years as a pastor, five years as a conference speaker. For most of those years I preached or taught over three hundred times a year. I know the incessant demand to deliver material that first would be true, and then be moving and witty and sometimes eloquent. I know that every waking moment for me was spent, one way or another, engaged in amassing material for sermons. Add to this counseling, personal witnessing, administrative responsibilities of running a church, and you have an overly full schedule.

With all of this, I found myself missing (or conveniently overlooking or justifying) growing signs of problems in my home. Cries for help from my family were drowned out by the roar of the demands of fulfilling my holy calling. When the cries ceased, I assumed the problem had been solved, but it was only that a death had occurred in my relationship with my wife. She now preferred a fantasy relationship with an imaginary lover over the real one she had with me. When I found out there was another man in her life, I was crushed. When the divorce came, I was shattered.

For seven long years I never preached or taught. The voice that had ministered to thousands was silenced. The ministry that had won hundreds to Christ, by his grace, was terminated. In those days, Bill, I know of no flaw in my devotion to Jesus. There was no extent to which my zeal for him was not willing to go. I was determined that the gifts God gave me would be used full bore. However, Bill, here's my point: Satan shrewdly turned my strengths into my weaknesses.

In my zeal to serve the Lord and effectively use the gifts that he gave me, everything else was viewed as competition and at cross-purposes with the goal I was consumed by. Please, I plead with you, don't let this happen to you. Spend time away from the demands of leadership. When someone points the finger of stinging criticism at you for being away from leadership, think of me. Determine you will not let your ministry and your dreams come crashing down around you like mine did around me. [1]

The busy life may cost you your marriage.

SOUL DISEASE

Chinese words are made up of characters. The individual meaning of the characters is combined to communicate the meaning of the word. The Chinese characters for the word "busy" are intriguing:

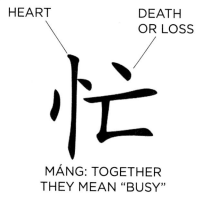

HEART

DEATH OR LOSS

MÁNG: TOGETHER THEY MEAN "BUSY"

Most people can relate to this meaning. When we live *day after day* in the busy, overwhelmed, burdened life with relationships that rarely go below the surface, we begin to feel a degree of loss or death in our hearts. If we live on this path for too long, our passion and zest for life feel like a distant memory.

Soul disease begins to set in and spread. We begin to make choices without regard to the things we will care about in the rocking chair. Much of the sinful behavior we witness can be connected to the effects of the busy life. Pastor and author John Ortberg writes:

Not long after moving to Chicago, I called a wise friend to ask for some spiritual direction. I described the pace of life in my current ministry. The church where I serve tends to move at a fast clip. I also told him about our rhythms of family life: we are in the van-driving, soccer-league, piano-lesson, school-orientation-night years. I told him about the present condition of my heart, as best I could discern it.

What did I need to do, I asked him, to be spiritually healthy?

Long pause. "You must ruthlessly eliminate hurry from your life," he said at last.

Another long pause.

"Okay, I've written that one down," I told him, a little impatiently. "That's a good one. Now, what else is there?" I had many things to do, and this was a long-distance call, so I was anxious to cram as many units of spiritual wisdom into the least amount of time possible.

Another long pause.

"There is nothing else," he said. "You must ruthlessly eliminate hurry from your life."

I've concluded that my life and the well-being of the people I serve depends on following his prescription, for hurry is the great enemy of spiritual life in our day. Hurry destroys souls. [2]

In the United States, more than six in ten Christians say that it's "often" or "always" true that "the busyness of life gets in the way of developing my relationship with God." [3]

In my spiritual life, the contrast between busy versus full is vivid as I seek to practice the presence of God. The Bible presents us with the opportunity to fellowship with the Living God. Remembering He is here with me, and interacting with Him feeds my soul like little else.

I consistently forget the reality of His presence when I am living the busy life, hurrying from one thing to the next. When I live the full life, my heart is nourished and strengthened by being "with Him." It harkens to the well-known contrast of Mary and Martha in Luke 10:38-42:

> As Jesus and his disciples were on their way, he came to a village where a woman named Martha opened her home to him. She had a sister called Mary, who sat at the Lord's feet listening to what he said. But Martha was distracted by all the preparations that had to be made. She came to him and asked, "Lord, don't you care that my sister has left me to do the work by myself? Tell her to help me!"
>
> "Martha, Martha," the Lord answered, "you are worried and upset about many things, but only one thing is needed. Mary has chosen what is better, and it will not be taken away from her."

I can follow in the footsteps of Mary or in the footsteps of Martha, relishing His presence or effectively forgetting *He is here.* I have a high degree of influence over the condition of my soul. My choices regarding pace of life are more significant than I may want to acknowledge.

The busy life may cost you the health of your soul.

THOSE CLOSEST TO US

Richard Swenson wrote in *The Overload Syndrome:*

> "Virtually all of our relationships are damaged by hurry. Many families are being starved to death by velocity. Our children lie wounded on the ground, run over by our high-speed good intentions." [3]

Consider Swenson's statement for a moment. How does "velocity" affect our relationships with those closest to us? If significant relationships thrive or decay based on meaningful time together, high-speed living is costly as it reduces our time connecting with one another to dangerously low levels.

In his book *Stress Fractures*, Chuck Swindoll shares:

I vividly remember some time back being caught in the undertow of too many commitments in too few days. It wasn't long before I was snapping at my wife and our children, choking down my food at mealtimes, and feeling irritated at those unexpected interruptions through the day. Before long, things around our home started reflecting the pattern of my hurry-up style. It was becoming unbearable.

I distinctly recall after supper one evening the words of our younger daughter, Colleen. She wanted to tell me about something important that had happened to her at school that day. She hurriedly began, "Daddy-I-wanna-tell-you-somethin'-and-I'll-tell-you-really-fast."

Suddenly realizing her frustration, I answered, "Honey, you can tell me . . . and you don't have to tell me really fast. Say it slowly."

I'll never forget her answer: "Then listen slowly." [4]

Who gets the brunt of the irritation, frustration, and criticism of the busy person? Normally, those closest to us. We typically hide the emotions we are not proud of from outsiders. We act friendly, giving the perception that everything is well so people we do not spend much time with will admire us.

It is ironic that we are most likely to vent the irritation and frustration of the hurried life on those whose admiration we will most care about at the end of our lives.

A classic "good intention" that may negatively affect our children is the desire to provide for our families. Some parents put it this way: "I want them to have what I did not." Others say, "We want financial security so each child can have his or her own bedroom, so we can afford the clothes that the other kids at school are wearing, and we can go on memorable vacations as a family."

A CLASSIC "GOOD INTENTION" THAT MAY NEGATIVELY AFFECT OUR CHILDREN IS THE DESIRE TO PROVIDE FOR OUR FAMILIES.

The desire to provide for our families is good. Sometimes, the "standard of living" we think is best for our families requires a job that keeps Dad at the office seventy hours a week. Sometimes, Mom and Dad both need to work to achieve this standard of living. Dad and Mom come home from a long and intense day at the office and have little left for the kids. Some parents have a work life where they are gone before their children awake and arrive home when the kids are in bed.

What is the impact if we aim for a standard of living that keeps us from daily quality, and quantity time, with our children? What could the busy life force us to say when we sit in the rocking chair?

In 1974, the song "Cat's in the Cradle" topped the Billboard Hot 100 as the most popular song in America. Harry Chapin wrote the song about his relationship with his son, Josh. The song comes from the mouth of a father who lives the busy life and never has time for his son.

While the son grows up, he asks his dad if they can spend time together. Dad responds "not now" but promises it will happen at some point in the future. The dad's inability to spend time with his son fails to tarnish the son's admiration for his father, "I'm gonna be like you Dad, You know I'm gonna be like you." Not surprisingly, the son eventually does become just like his father and the father experiences what the son must have felt growing up.

Before you read the lyrics, it is significant to note Chapin weaves nursery rhymes into the song that highlight the two sides of the story. On one side we have "the cat in the cradle," representing the family being at home together. On the other side we find the "silver spoon," signifying the wealth that the dad must leave his family to pursue.

Back at home, we see the "little boy blue," the son who is sad because he cannot have what he most wants from his father—time together. Far away from home, there is the "man on the moon," the dad who is unreachable and yet still a hero to the boy. [5]

Take a minute to read through the lyrics. I have an unusual request—listen to the song while you read. With its popularity, you should have no trouble finding the song on YouTube or another site:

My child arrived just the other day
He came to the world in the usual way
But there were planes to catch and bills to pay
He learned to walk while I was away
And he was talkin' 'fore I knew it, and as he grew
He'd say "I'm gonna be like you dad
You know I'm gonna be like you"

And the cat's in the cradle and the silver spoon
Little boy blue and the man on the moon
When you comin' home dad?
I don't know when, but we'll get together then
You know we'll have a good time then

My son turned ten just the other day

He said, "Thanks for the ball, Dad, come on let's play

Can you teach me to throw", I said "Not today

I got a lot to do", he said, "That's ok"

And he walked away but his smile never dimmed

And said, "I'm gonna be like him, yeah

You know I'm gonna be like him"

And the cat's in the cradle and the silver spoon

Little boy blue and the man on the moon

When you comin' home dad?

I don't know when, but we'll get together then

You know we'll have a good time then

Well, he came from college just the other day

So much like a man I just had to say

"Son, I'm proud of you, can you sit for a while?"

He shook his head and he said with a smile

"What I'd really like, Dad, is to borrow the car keys

See you later, can I have them please?"

And the cat's in the cradle and the silver spoon

Little boy blue and the man on the moon

When you comin' home son?

I don't know when, but we'll get together then dad

You know we'll have a good time then

I've long since retired, my son's moved away

I called him up just the other day

I said, "I'd like to see you if you don't mind"

He said, "I'd love to, Dad, if I can find the time

You see my new job's a hassle and kids have the flu

But it's sure nice talking to you, Dad

It's been sure nice talking to you"

And as I hung up the phone it occurred to me

He'd grown up just like me

My boy was just like me

And the cat's in the cradle and the silver spoon

Little boy blue and the man on the moon

When you comin' home son?

I don't know when, but we'll get together then Dad

You know we'll have a good time then. [6]

Chapin remarked of his ballad, "Frankly, this song scares me to death." [7] The song was immediately popular and has remained so over time because it captures a phenomenon that all of us fear will happen to us. Our fears are not unfounded.

The struggle between time with our families and the need to provide a living and "get stuff done" is not easy for anyone. Yet, if we fail on this point, choosing to-do lists and a preoccupation with work over time nurturing relationships with loved ones, will we not end up filled with immense regret in the rocking chair? May God help us never sing this song with our lives.

The busy life will cost you in the relationships with those closest to you.

· · · · · · ·

If you are reading this and your kids are grown and you feel you've already failed on this point, may I suggest a course of action? As we discussed previously, a ninety-degree heading change in anyone's life is noticeable.

What if you immediately began to make choices valuing time fully present with people more than everything that is less important? What if you called your grown kids and expressed your regret and your commitment to spend the rest of your life putting a high value on them?

It is possible your radical course change would have reverberating effects on all your relationships and in the lives of everyone you love. Your testimony at the end of your life could be different from this day forward. ∎

CHAPTER SEVEN REVIEW & SMALL GROUP QUESTIONS

1. In this chapter, we talked about how people treat busyness in their lives like a pet golden retriever rather than a cobra. Have you seen this happen in someone else's life? How about in your own life?

\
\
\
\
\
\

2. Look back over the letter to Bill Hybels from the former pastor. Which statement in his letter do you find most surprising? Why?

\
\
\
\
\
\

3. Can you think of a season in your life when busyness has contributed to "soul disease" —hurting the health of your walk with the Lord?

\
\
\
\
\
\

4. Dr. Richard Swenson stated that many children are being "run over" by the pace of life in their home. How prevalent is this phenomenon today? What do you think is the first step toward addressing the situation?

_____

_____

_____

_____

_____

_____

5. The father in "Cat's In The Cradle" neglected his relationship with his son because of his job and pursuit of wealth. What pulls you away from the kind of relationship you want with your children (or loved ones)?

_____

_____

_____

_____

_____

_____

CHAPTER EIGHT

AIMING FOR FULL

*Insanity is doing the same thing over and over
and expecting different results.*

— Albert Einstein

D id Jesus live busy or full? Reflect on Jesus' example for a minute. He had at least as many things on His plate as any one of us. His assignment: show people what God the Father is like, usher in the Kingdom of God, find and develop a core group of leaders to take the gospel to the ends of the earth, redeem all humanity, and prove His identity via the resurrection—all in three years.

He must have felt the temptation to live the busy life. So how did Jesus live? Imagine this scene:

Jesus hurriedly goes over to a sleeping Peter, wakes him, and gives him a cup of coffee, notepad, and pen.

"Peter! Come on sleepyhead, it's five o'clock in the morning. We need to get moving. There are things to do and people to heal. The rooster's gonna be crowing before we know it."

Peter yawns, stretches, and mutters "Mmm-hmm, yes Sir."

THE VIEW FROM THE ROCKING CHAIR

Jesus sees Peter is almost ready, begins pacing back and forth, and fires away, "First, we have to cut down on healings that aren't in the program. They are reducing our efficiency, and efficiency is KEY.

"Second, a few of the disciples have been dropping behind the group when we walk to the different towns. Everyone must keep up. We are only as strong as the weakest link. Maybe we need to start an exercise program.

"Third, we need a new navigator. We've not been taking the most direct route from town to town; I keep telling you guys, I've only got three years to get all this stuff done.

"Fourth, people have been asking about what I said on the Mount last week—you know, that briefing that sort of turned into a sermon? I don't have time to repeat that so I need you and a couple of the others to copy down what I said in bullet form and hand it out when people ask for it.

"Last, I'm going for a jog and will have my prayer time while I run so I can kill two birds with one stone. I'd like you to have the boys briefed by the time I get back and then we'll get going for the day. Got it? Get yourself another cup of coffee and let's get movin'! Ready—break!!!"

While it may be humorous to think about it, is this the picture we see in the gospels? Not quite. How do we see Jesus answering the question of busy or full? I think we can agree that Jesus' life provides a compelling picture of the full life.

If you think Jesus was in a hurry, remember the time when Jesus was headed to the synagogue ruler's house to heal the man's daughter. A woman who had been sick for twelve years reached out to touch him in hopes that He might heal her. When she covertly touched Jesus, she was instantly healed but the healing did not go unnoticed.

Jesus stopped the throng traveling with him to acknowledge what had happened and why it had happened: "Daughter, your faith has healed you. Go in peace."

Jesus' highest value in this encounter was not efficiency. If so, He might have pressed on to his next appointment without acknowledging her. Instead, He stopped and recognized this woman, sealing her relationship with Him. Jesus always seemed right on pace and exactly where He wanted to be.

JESUS AND EFFICIENCY

If you still think Jesus was primarily task-oriented and all about efficiency, consider the way Jesus treated children.

When children approached Jesus, the disciples tried to keep them away like the Secret Service keeps shady characters away from the President. From the disciples' perspective, children were the last people who would help the cause of bringing Christ's Kingdom. Adults—lots of adults—influential people were the best targets for His message. Children were a waste of the Master's time. Jesus' disciples were operating out of a mindset we sometimes have today. We think that living strategic, intentional lives means being task-oriented with unswerving efficiency. Christ's life debunks this thinking.

Note Jesus' reaction to His disciples' treatment of the children. Jesus was "indignant" with His disciples for keeping the children from Him. Jesus rebuked His inner circle, saying, *"Let the little children come to me, and do not hinder them, for the kingdom of God belongs to such as these."* —Mark 10:14

Jesus made time to lift the little children into his arms and bless them. Jesus relished, and did not rush, these encounters.

JESUS AND DISTRACTIONS

If you think Jesus was distracted, recall the night before His crucifixion. He gathered with His disciples for a lengthy Passover dinner, reclining at the table with them. He took a towel and washbasin and washed each of His followers' feet while Judas was organizing the betrayal.

Jesus gave them detailed instructions about the coming of the Holy Spirit and encouragement for what they were about to face. He invited the disciples to pray fervently through the night with Him. In the face of the coming torture and execution, Jesus' behavior offers no evidence that He was distracted. Instead, we see Him fully present.

This was how He lived His entire life on earth. Jesus illustrated the full life better than anyone else in history. What were His motivations for living this way?

THE CHARACTER AND VALUES OF GOD

Zoom out to the 30,000-foot level for a moment. The more we understand the character and values of God and align ourselves with them, the more prepared we are to answer the questions of life (e.g. Am I aiming for busy or full?).

When we look at three of the epic acts of God—the creation of humankind, the essence of the Gospel, and God's plan for our eternity—what value is most dramatically apparent?

- *God created Adam and Eve and walked and talked to them in the garden; they were in unbroken relationship with Him.* —Genesis 1:27-28; 3:8

- *Jesus came to live among us and die for us to restore the parent-child relationship with God we were created to have. Because of the Gospel, we can call Him Abba or Daddy.* — Romans 8:15

- *For all of eternity, we will not need the sun anymore because we will be living in the light of God's glory—in intimate relationship with Him. —Revelation 21:3, 23*

God highly values relationship.

Relationships require time. Notice how Jesus built relationships with His disciples—relationships He knew would be tested up to the point of death. He did not ask them to come by to study the Old Testament every Sunday morning for an hour. He told the fishermen, "Come follow Me and I will make you fishers of men."

He asked them to drop their nets and leave their old lives behind so they could come live with Him twenty-four/seven.

Jesus planned for the disciples to spend all their time with Him so they could learn to trust Him and become like Him. The night before He was crucified, Jesus taught His disciples how His relationship with them would continue to grow through the constant presence of the Holy Spirit who would be sent to them later:

"If anyone loves me, he will obey my teaching. My Father will love him, and we will come to him and make our home with him." —John 14:23

If your mother-in-law calls and exclaims she is coming to "make her home with you," you would not be alone if your heart skipped a beat. Whether she is your favorite or least favorite person on the planet, you would know life was about to change dramatically, because you would be spending a lot of time with her.

God intends for our relationship with Him to be like He is moving into the house with us. Relationship in His mind equals regular, constant time together. We have a hard time getting our minds around this when it comes to God. Nonetheless, it is His desire to fellowship with us continually.

THE MOST SIGNIFICANT EQUATION

Jesus loved His disciples so He spent time with them. He demonstrated a concept that has become veiled to many parents and children alike. It is summed up in an "equation" that is more significant than anything you ever learned in school. Here it is:

$$LOVE = TIME$$

If you want a deep and meaningful relationship with your spouse, child, sibling, or parent, express your "love" by spending time with them. If you feel like this equation is a blinding flash of the obvious, you are not alone.

Rocket scientists, Super Bowl MVPs, and Fortune 500 executives can adeptly determine the best course of action in very complex scenarios. Yet, their relationships strongly indicate a rejection or ignorance of this simple equation.

There are many ways you can spend that time and some ways are better than others. But ultimately, it is critical to acknowledge this: Loving relationships are fundamentally built on time together. (In later chapters, we will offer ideas of valuable ways to spend time together with loved ones.)

TIME AND TEENAGERS

Many parents doubt the veracity of this equation, especially as their children reach adolescence. Their fourteen-year-old wants to play softball, run track, be in the play, play an instrument in the recital, attend camp, and spend the rest of her time with her five BFFs ("Best Friends Forever" for the non-texters).

Already strapped for time, the parents convince themselves that time together with their teens is a luxury rather than a necessity.

Donna Cox is a homemaker, high school teacher, and speaker who has led seminars for teenagers and parents for more than a decade. Listen to what she has learned:

> *As a high school teacher, I often have the opportunity to engage students in writing activities that allow me to look into their very heart. I ask them to journal on this topic: "Is it still important to have your parents presence in your life now that you are a teenager?" Almost every student expresses an intense desire to have their parents involved in their world. They wish that their parents would go to the sporting events, wish they would ask them about their day, wish they knew about who they were dating and what they loved to do.*
>
> *As a seminar leader, I have come to this conclusion: Children need you the most the first few years of their life, then they need you just as much during their teen years. If you invest time in your teenager, IT WILL PAY OFF in the end. It's like money in the bank if you just invest that time.* [1]

Just shy of his thirtieth birthday, a friend of mine felt a deep lack of fulfillment after years of pleasure-seeking. All the world had to offer hadn't brought him any real meaning or happiness.

One day, as we talked, he said, "I never really knew my dad until I was eighteen." Materially, my friend had it all while growing up. Massive houses, dream vacations, nice cars. But the cost of wealth was a dad who never had time for his son. He would have traded everything for a meaningful relationship with his dad.

Surrounded by stuff and missing a relationship with his father, my friend came to believe pleasure was his purpose. Experimenting with drugs and chasing women brought pleasure so he jumped in with both feet.

My friend's honest look in the mirror revealed a picture that he did not like. When I asked what he wanted to change, the quality of his relationship with his dad was at the top of the list.

There are some crucial questions we need to ask and answer. What do my spouse and children need most from me? Is it the truth or a lie that my wife (or husband) and kids need a big home filled with the latest and greatest toys, Disneyland vacations, and all the extras?

At the end of their lives, will they be relishing the memories of all that *stuff* or regretting that they never really knew their dad, or mom, because he or she never had the time?

SINCE WE ARE FOLLOWERS OF JESUS ...

If you are a Christ-follower, you are invited, even commanded, to live just as He did. The deepest motivation, greatest license, and most compelling force to live the full life, in the midst of a culture that venerates the busy life, is your love for God and His call on your life to live like Christ.

Jesus' call to "Follow me" invites us to follow the rhythm and relational ways of our Master.

The world, maybe our friends, and possibly even those in the Church may not reward you for living full instead of busy. You may be ridiculed and deserted by those who do not appreciate and understand. But those who you will care about most at the end of your life will be forever grateful.

TWO STORIES

Looking at examples of how others thoughtfully and courageously answer the question of "busy versus full" can provide additional inspiration.

We know a physician that developed a successful family practice over the first fifteen years of his career. During that time, he and his wife had five children within eight years. Building and maintaining his practice required between 70 – 80 hours each week. After wrestling with the question of busy versus full, he counted the cost of maintaining the status quo and determined that cost was too high.

This physician closed one part of his practice in order to dramatically reduce the time away from his wife and children. As expected, the decision resulted in a 40% reduction in their family income. Added to this, his decision was unpopular with many of his patients as well as a few physician colleagues. But his compelling response to all his patients and everyone who asked was, "I want my kids to know their Dad."

My wife and I have another friend who went to an Ivy League university and law school. When he graduated from law school, he was courted and hired by a large national law firm that compensates their lawyers extremely well. He worked at the firm for several years on a partnership track, regularly working sixty to sixty-five hours per week. The firm made clear the expectation that he would continue working this many hours each week until his retirement.

> HE REDUCED HIS SALARY . . . BUT GAINED TWENTY HOURS A WEEK FOR DECADES.

After some soul searching, my friend decided to leave the law firm to take a job as an attorney with a federal agency. In doing so, he reduced his salary and retirement package by *two-thirds*.

The government agency requires my friend to work forty to forty-five hours each week. He turned down a career path on which he could have made a lot more money, but he has gained twenty hours a week for the next two or three decades.

My friend uses this time to nurture his relationship with his wife and children, to help his family grow in godliness, and to lead mission trips in the church and ministries in the local community. His life looks very different than it might have without this course change—and he has no regrets.

SIX PRACTICAL WAYS TO AIM FOR THE FULL LIFE

How do we live the full life like Jesus did? Consider these six practical ways to replace busy with full:

KNOW YOUR NON-NEGOTIABLES

There are many things we want to happen in our lives. We may want to be physically fit, have children who excel academically, sing in the choir, or climb all the fourteeners in Colorado.

There are things we want to happen, but if they don't, we could live with it. If someone came along and made us the right offer, we would potentially give these away to get something better. These are the negotiables of life.

There are also things in our lives that we not only want to happen, but as far as it depends on us, they *must* happen. These things are at the core of what we believe it means to be successful in this life. Regardless of what someone offered us, these things could never be negotiated away. These are the "non-negotiables" of life.

What are your non-negotiables? What are the things you want to happen during this life that could never be negotiated away from you at any price? As you sit in the rocking chair at the end of your life, what will have needed to happen for you to look back with the deepest satisfaction?

Build your life around accomplishing these things. Pour the first, greatest, and best of your life into these things. The negotiables of life can get the leftovers.

If the negotiables do not get finished or finished well, that is acceptable. You will have the fulfillment, peace, and passion that come when you give your best to the things that are most important.

SCHEDULE FIRST WHAT MATTERS MOST

Most people feel the tug of what seems to be a never-ending list of requests, opportunities, and commitments. We can subtly fall prey to deceptive thinking: I can do it all, be it all, and have it all.

Jesus knew we needed Him to clarify things for us: *"Seek first the Kingdom of God and His righteousness [His right ways of living.]"* —Matthew 6:33, NKJV

One key step in living this out is scheduling first what matters most. Take your calendar before it has anything else on it, except for the mandatory requirements of work and school, and block out time for the activities that will bring about your non-negotiables.

For example, consider putting these kinds of things on your calendar: study God's Word every morning at six o'clock, sit on the couch with my spouse without the TV each night at nine, read a stack of books with my three-year-old before naptime, go on a walk each Thursday after work with my teenage daughter, memorize a verse of Scripture as a family at the end of dinner, play our favorite family board game every Friday night, invite a single-parent family over for dinner one Saturday each month.

When our daily, weekly, and monthly calendars are filled with seeking first God's Kingdom and His way of life, we experience the joy of seeing the most important things being lived out day by day.

EMPLOY THE POWER OF ROUTINE

Making a good decision will cost you something. Every time you carefully consider alternatives for how to spend your time, you expend the cost (time and energy) to receive the benefit (positive movement toward a goal). When we establish a routine as a result of a good decision, it generates a recurring benefit but we only have to pay the cost the first time.

We know routines work for things like brushing your teeth. However, many people fear that routines in the spiritual or relational realm will make things dry and lifeless.

Our experience has been just the opposite. Routines can enhance our relationships and develop family 'momentum' in the right direction.

Look at the activities on your calendar that help accomplish your non-negotiables and bring richness to your life. Consider which of these you can make part of your daily or weekly family routine.

ONE THING AT A TIME

Multitasking is necessary.

Being married to a homeschooling mother of six has convinced me there are times when you have to devote your time and attention to multiple people and tasks. Yet, most homeschooling moms and high-level executives agree that life is most enjoyable—and their best work is completed—when focusing on one thing at a time.

Brain research has actually proven that true multitasking is impossible. Although this concept may shock some people, the brain can only concentrate on one thing at a time. We are wired by God to resist multitasking.

Many people find themselves dividing their attention, not because they have to, but because requests for their attention come within a short span of time. This reality may tempt us but should not compel us to multitask.

Some of us have made efficiency a higher value than relationship. We make cell phone calls while going through the drive-thru, not because we have to, but because we will accomplish more on our lists. We accept treating the drive-thru attendant like an ATM because our lists have to get done.

Commit to focusing on one person or one thing at a time, whenever possible. Consider it a discipline that you are determined to master. This opens the door to living life *fully present* in every situation. As you focus on one thing at a time, you will be more likely to see what God wants you to see, do what He wants you to do, and give your best to whomever you are with—out of love for Him and others. Everyone wins when we live this way.

EVERY YES MEANS A NO

If you are a "time optimist," this point may be difficult to accept. In micro-economics, they teach you about "opportunity cost." Opportunity cost means that every opportunity I commit to costs me all the other things I could have been participating in during that specific timeframe. Another way of expressing this is, "Every yes means a no."

Each time you schedule something, you must acknowledge you have just said no to doing other things. You have committed some of your time and energy resources so your available time and energy for the rest of life is diminished. While this may seem intuitive, many people would say living with this in mind is elusive.

Failure to understand opportunity cost results in "the busy life" as we have described it. But remembering that *every yes means a no* will help you live more carefully, thoughtfully, and prayerfully as new opportunities and requests arrive at your doorstep.

RETHINK "SABBATH"

Many are scared of the idea of Sabbath because it smells of legalism and it seems almost impossible to put into practice. Before we allow the cultural bias against Sabbath to win the day, remember Jesus said, "The Sabbath was made for man, not man for the Sabbath."

Remember God modeled the rhythm of work and then rest. Remember God did not suggest we rest; He commanded it. Remember that failing to observe a rhythm of work and rest may contribute to finding our identity in our work instead of our relationships—particularly our relationship with Him.

A legalistic practice of a Sabbath is a bad idea. Embracing a day aimed at rest, rejuvenation, and refocusing on what is most important is a powerful idea. Attempt to make this practical element a life-giving habit for your family.

. . . .

These six practical points can help us filter our choices. If we keep these in view each day, we can structure our time and commitments based on the most important things. Take a moment and reflect on each point.

Which one could be most valuable to you when making decisions? Which will help you stay on course and get to the rocking chair without regrets?

YOUR COMPASS CHECK

Now that the first question—Am I aiming for busy or full?—is fresh in your mind, we want to provide a chance for you to begin work on your "Compass Check." Remember, the Compass Check is a set of questions that help you check the compass of your life so you arrive at your desired destination.

Keep in mind the need to develop both "check-up" questions and "filter" questions.

Check-up questions allow you to see if you are on course. For example:

> *In the last week, have I been living busy or full?*

> *If I replicate the amount of time I spent with my kids last week, what will they say about our relationship in the rocking chair?*

Filter questions help you stay on course when new opportunities arise. For example:

> *If every yes means a no, what might this activity actually cost us?*

> *Would saying "yes" to this fragment our family or bring us together?*

This is brainstorming and not a final draft, so write down any questions that seem reasonable. Reviewing your answers to the Rocking Chair exercise (page 27) may help generate questions.

What question(s) could you regularly ask yourself to see if you are on course related to the question "Am I aiming for busy or full?" What question(s) would help you make wise choices and stay on course when new opportunities arise? What question(s) would help you make choices in light of your answers to the Rocking Chair exercise? What question(s) would help you guard against things that have pulled you "off course" in the past (i.e. working late, too much time online)? Write your questions below.

_____

_____

_____

_____

_____

_____

_____

_____

_____

_____

_____

In the final chapter of this book, we will take the necessary steps to finalize your Compass Check—a tool I believe you will find effective and eternally valuable. ∎

CHAPTER EIGHT REVIEW & SMALL GROUP QUESTIONS

1. How would you describe the pace of life Jesus modeled for us in the gospels?

_____

_____

_____

_____

_____

_____

_____

2. What are some stories or passages in the Bible that show God highly values relationship?

_____

_____

_____

_____

_____

_____

_____

3. As discussed in the chapter, many people focus more on providing nice homes, cars, and clothes for their loved ones than on developing strong relationships with them. What is most important for you to provide for your spouse and children (or loved ones)?

_____

_____

_____

_____

_____

_____

_____

4. What are your non-negotiables?

_____

_____

_____

_____

_____

_____

_____

5. Which of the "Six Practical Ways to Aim for Full" do you think could be most helpful to you?

_____

_____

_____

_____

_____

_____

_____

CHAPTER NINE

ARE WE AIMING FOR GOOD OR GODLY?

*The family is the cornerstone of our society. More than any
other force, it shapes the attitude, the hopes, the ambitions,
and the values of the child.*

— Lyndon Baines Johnson

A single man in graduated studies titled his first doctoral thesis, "Five Definitive Principles On Parenting." Five years later, when the same man had married and had his first child, he was asked by a local university to update and present his thesis. He did so but only after re-titling his work, "Five Principles On Parenting."

Five years later, the same man, who now had four children, was again asked to present his thesis material. This time he titled it, "Five Random Thoughts On Parenting."

Three years later, after the same man had his fifth child, he was once again asked to present his material. He changed the title one final time to, "Help, I'm Drowning!" [1]

Parenting is truly one of the most humorous and humbling endeavors on the planet. The second question we will use to check our compass relates to our aim in parenting: "Are we aiming for good or are we aiming for godly?"

For this question to be valuable, we need to carefully define our terms.

Good—meeting societal expectations, behavior that is in bounds, reflecting the character and highest values of our culture

Godly—like God, reflecting God's character and highest values

Before we go farther into what can be a sensitive area of parenting, there are a few things I want to say. There is a good chance you are reading this book because you care a great deal about this question. You care deeply about seeing your children walk with the Lord. At the end of your life, one of the first things you will think about as you sit in the rocking chair is the type of relationship your kids have with the Lord.

It is hard for Christian parents to contemplate sitting in that rocking chair, filled with gratitude, peace, and joy if their children have shunned the faith that they have tried to pass on to them. For parents, I believe the direction and destination of our children's lives are close to the center of the target for all of us.

And yet, we recognize we do not have as much control in this area as we would like. In parenting, we sometimes feel that we would like to have complete control. We would like our children's decisions to be completely up to us. We would like to have a straightforward, unchanging formula for raising them successfully. Simply add A to B and you will get C—a perfect child—each and every time.

But there is no formula to raising a perfect child. I think God did this on purpose. If there were a formula, we would focus on it instead of focusing on Him. We would be less likely to draw upon His strength. We would not need to continually seek His wisdom. We would probably take things into our own hands and put the formula into practice without Him.

So He does not give us a formula. But He does give us precepts, promises, and provision. He offers precepts from His Word to live out and teach. He promises us that our lives as parents will make a deep imprint on our children. And He offers the provision of His strength, courage, and wisdom through the presence of His Spirit.

His promise to be with us always is incredibly heartening as we seek to make Christ-followers out of our own children.

WHAT WE SEE

So how are things working out? The headlines are not encouraging. Multiple studies conducted during the last twenty years have found that two out of three teenagers who grew up going to church stop being involved in church life as they transition to adulthood. [2] Once they graduate from high school, it seems they also graduate from their faith in Christ.

In light of this reality, we should ask ourselves why this phenomenon is so prevalent. While we shouldn't oversimplify this complex issue or make one aspect of teen life the scapegoat, I believe part of the answer may lie in the difference between good and godly.

EVIDENCE FOR GODLY

At this point, let's take a quick look at Scripture to see what God has planned for everyone who follows Him.

In Romans 8:29, we see we are predestined to be conformed to the *"likeness of his Son."* In Colossians 3:9-10, we learn we have taken off the old self with its practices and put on the new self that is *"being renewed in knowledge in the image of its Creator."* In Ephesians 4:22-24, we discover that we have put off the old self and have put on the new self, *"created to be like God in true righteousness and holiness."*

In Galatians 4:19, we find out that Christ is being formed in us. Second Corinthians 3:18 tells us that we are *"being transformed into His likeness with ever-increasing glory."*

The picture is like a Colorado mountain stream—crystal clear.

God's design for His people is unmistakable—that we be like Him. Yet, the contrast between good and godly may not be as clear when we think about raising children. For this reason, let's do the following exercise:

First, find a quiet place to work on this exercise. Review the definitions for good and godly at the start of this chapter. Next, list some of the things "good kids" do. Then, try to describe the corresponding behavior for kids who are aiming for godly. We have provided a few examples.

GOOD   GODLY

GOOD	GODLY
Get good grades	Work with all their hearts for God
Stay out of trouble	Pursue righteousness, love, and peace
Focus on outward behavior	Focus on the heart

You can download and print this exercise at www.sonrisemountainranch.org/exercises/good_vs_godly.

Here are some answers we've gathered from Christian parents across the United States:

GOOD GODLY

GOOD	GODLY
Get good grades	Work with all their hearts for God
Are well-rounded—have a good résumé for college	Seek first God's Kingdom and righteousness
Develop their gifts and skills to the max	Develop gifts as they serve God
Focus on outward behavior	Focus on the heart
Act differently depending on who they are with	Act the same regardless of who they are with
Know how to be polite and engaging	Are genuinely thoughtful
Have a sense of entitlement	Live in gratitude and contentment
Keep out of trouble	Pursue righteousness
Get wrapped up in dating	Prepare for a Godly marriage
Talk about God and go to church	Talk with God and live for the Lord

Review your answers and the responses from other Christian parents. This exercise begins to illuminate the significance of our aim in parenting. Many of us have used both "good" and "godly" to describe our children and not considered the distinction.

At first glance, the two appear very similar. Yet, the closer we look, the more differences we see. It may remind you of the lesson of the compass. The seemingly small divergence of ten degrees in our aim will equate to a different destination—in this case, different character traits and values in our children when they leave our home.

Since the direction of our children means so much to us, now and at the end of our lives, let us continue to investigate the contrast.

SIX EYE-OPENING DIFFERENCES

Let's take a closer look at six contrasts from the "Good vs. Godly" exercise.

Good kids get good grades.
Godly kids work with all their hearts.

Good kids think their grades are important because their parents tell them so. Good grades will get them into a good college. A prestigious college will mean a good job. A well-paying job will lead to a happy retirement. A happy retirement is the mark of a successful life. The American Dream has been achieved. (More on the American Dream in Chapter Twelve.)

If we drill into our kids that good grades are the first domino of many in achieving a successful life, can you imagine the pressure they might feel? Perhaps this sheds light on why between seventy-five and ninety-eight percent of college students surveyed each year report having cheated in high school. [3]

Godly kids recognize grades have meaning, but make it their goal to work with all their heart for God's glory (Colossians 3:23). They trust in God's guidance and provision for the future. Godly kids know that getting an A in a class does not necessarily mean you worked with all your heart. Conversely, getting a C+ can be just as pleasing as an A if you exerted maximum effort for God's pleasure and honor.

Good kids aim to be well-rounded.
Godly kids seek first God's Kingdom and righteousness.

Good kids believe they need to be well-rounded. The new Oxford-American dictionary defines this as, "fully developed in all areas." Such development takes an immense amount of time and training.

Piano lessons, soccer practice, dance lessons, baseball practice, and drama rehearsals make for a busy existence—an unfortunate but necessary cost of making "well-rounded" a high value. One or two practices a week is normally not enough to reach "fully developed."

Good kids may observe one thing while being expected to believe another. If we create our family schedule around the development of our child, sacrificing other things so they can attend all the practices and rehearsals, and then tell them their lives are not about themselves but about Jesus, can you see how that might be hard for them to believe?

Godly kids believe expanding God's Kingdom and living in His ways is their primary target. They fight against being self-centered and trust that they will find the greatest joy and purpose in living for others. They see sports and other extracurricular activities as an opportunity to grow in godly character and influence others for the Lord.

Good kids have a sense of entitlement.
Godly kids live in gratitude and contentment.

Good kids think often about their wants and needs. Clothing, toys, technology, entertainment—happiness is directly related to attaining these things. Therefore, these things are essentially a right and something deserved, especially if they're being "good."

Good kids discover that regardless of what they already have, they would still like more—more stuff, friends, and vacations. It seems like a thirst that can never be quenched.

You may be surprised to learn that at a time when children enjoy more material wealth than ever before, they suffer from some of the highest depression and suicide rates ever known. [4]

Godly kids trust that God will provide what they need and

see the good things they receive as gifts. Accordingly, they aim to live with the attitude of gratitude. They choose not to see material possessions as the path to contentment. They understand that what they need most from their parents is relationship and guidance more than stuff.

Good kids speak and act differently.
Godly kids speak and act the same.

Good kids know their audience and act accordingly. They may be polite and engaging when talking to a friend's parents, while unkind and uninterested when siblings address them. They may appear to have several modes—school mode, church mode, sibling mode, friend mode—that are all noticeably different.

Godly kids choose their words and actions in light of God's Word. They aim to be equally kind and loving in what they say and how they act with their family, friends, and strangers. They are the same regardless of the setting. They strive to grow in integrity.

Good kids get immersed in dating.
Godly kids prepare for a godly marriage.

Good kids see dating as a natural part of the teen years and a path to entertainment and pleasure. Once dating begins, good kids often become consumed with thinking about these relationships and may lose interest in other pursuits, hobbies, or friends. Much of the discussion and drama in their lives centers on who they are dating, who they want to date, or who they just broke up with.

Godly kids understand that God's primary purpose for the romantic relationship has to do with godly marriage. Consequently, they limit the amount of time and energy thinking about romantic relationships until the appropriate season. They think of those of the opposite sex as brothers or sisters rather than romantic interests.

They strive to develop the kind of selfless character and wholesome thought life that will prepare them to be a godly husband or wife.

Teen dating is a potential off-ramp from godly to good. When a Christian young person goes from red-hot for Jesus to lukewarm in a short period of time, we have regularly observed that a romantic relationship is involved. It is heartbreaking for parents to see strong devotion to the Lord replaced by intense devotion to a boyfriend or girlfriend.

Studies show that three out of four students who date through high school participate in some form of sex. [5] This opens the door to sexting, STDs, unwanted pregnancy, abortion, teen dating violence, and rape. The current teen statistics on these issues are startling and sad. [6] Many parents are unsure of how to help their children navigate these challenging waters. For resources on this topic, see Appendix A.

Good kids talk about God and go to church.
Godly kids talk with God and live for the Lord.

Good kids are sometimes hard to distinguish from a committed follower of Jesus because they will talk about God in certain settings and may even attend church or youth group regularly. But many times, when they hear God's Word, they have doubts about what may happen if they put it into practice.

When making choices, good kids feel the tension between pleasure (what they want) and godliness, so they feel as if they are sitting on a fence—with one leg dangled on either side. They may fear surrendering their life to God will mean a loss of all things fun and will result in being labeled a "Jesus freak."

Good kids may appear godly for a season when hard times come. They may pray for God's assistance or offer obedience in return for His intervention. But when the difficulty is over, good kids return to life as it was before. In short, good kids live for their own desires rather than the things of God.

Godly kids talk to God as their perfect Father who loves them without fail. They believe He is trustworthy in all things, so they see becoming like Him and obeying His Word as the path to the greatest life—not second best.

Godly kids experience the peace and joy of knowing they have surrendered control to God. They desire for others to experience what they have and do not fear being called names because they love Jesus.

> THEY SEE BECOMING LIKE HIM AND OBEYING HIS WORD AS THE PATH TO THE GREATEST LIFE—NOT SECOND BEST.

Godly kids go to church and youth group to learn, be encouraged, and serve others—but you can see their love for God in how they live all week long.

With our "Good vs. Godly" exercise completed, it is time for an honest assessment. What do you see in the kids who attend your church? What do you see in your own children? Which do you think is the norm today?

The story of one famous family in the Old Testament spotlights the greatest threat to our children when it comes to aiming for godly.

THE GREATEST THREAT

In 1 Corinthians 10:11, we discover the intended purpose of many Old Testament stories for our lives today: *"These things happened to them [people in the Old Testament] as examples and were written down as warnings for us."*

The story of King David does not begin like a warning and, for a long time, does not even give us a hint that his example will be used as an admonition. But his story is crucial for those who care about the question of good versus godly.

Bruce Wilkinson provides a classic summary of King David and his children:

David was a Renaissance Man before the Renaissance. King, warrior, poet, musician, philosopher, politician, architect . . . He seemed to excel at everything he put his hand to . . . except parenting. Despite his close relationship to his Father in heaven, David was a miserable father to his own children here on earth. The royal princes lived hedonistic lives that were out of control. The evidence:

David's oldest son raped his half-sister and left her a "desolate woman."

Though David was "furious," he did nothing.

When the girl's other brother murdered the brother who raped her, David did nothing.

When the son who had murdered his brother returned from his self-imposed exile, David would not meet or speak to him for two years.

As this son's resentment towards his father grew, he planned and executed an overthrow of his father's kingdom.

Later, two other sons competed for the throne, and the struggled ended in one having the other killed. [7]

David is described as *"a man after God's own heart."* —1 Samuel 13:14 When I read some of the psalms he wrote, I can only imagine what his prayer life must have been like. But when we consider his amazing devotion to the Lord and his heartbreaking family life, it forces us to ask, "How did David's family get there?"

We find one clue buried in what seems to be an unimportant list of King David's managers found in 1 Chronicles 27:30-33:

> *Obil the Ishmaelite was in charge of the camels.*
> *Jehdeiah the Meronothite was in charge of the donkeys.*
> *Jaziz the Hagrite was in charge of the flocks...*
> *Jonathan, David's uncle, was a counselor, a man of insight and a scribe.*
> *Jehiel son of Hacmoni took care of the king's sons.*
> *Ahithophel was the king's counselor.*

Jehiel took care of David's sons. Why? David and all the Israelites probably felt David had more important things to do. There were decrees to make and nations to conquer. David decided to "outsource" the training and instruction of his children.

He abdicated his God-given role in their lives and he, along with the entire nation of Israel, paid for it dearly. Outsourcing is *the greatest threat* to families who are aiming for godly instead of good. Busyness is outsourcing's willing accomplice.

> OUTSOURCING IS THE GREATEST THREAT TO FAMILIES WHO ARE AIMING FOR GODLY INSTEAD OF GOOD.

Most Christian parents believe the primary role of teaching their kids about God and his ways belongs to the pastor, youth leader, and Sunday school teacher. This comes in the form of three common beliefs we as parents may hold:

1. "The pastor and church workers are the professionals—the ones who understand the Bible and can teach it the best."

Our culture encourages us to "leave it to the professionals." whenever possible. We are likely to accept this because we suspect that our own Bible knowledge is inferior to that of ministry professionals.

2. "The pastor and his staff have time and energy to teach my children and I do not."

If you have a hectic schedule to begin with, it can be overwhelming to think of being the main source of spiritual instruction to your kids. It feels like one more thing added to the "To Do" list.

3. "Don't we give money to the church so the staff and workers can provide the Bible training our children need?"

Some Christians feel better about their contribution to the church if they see a return on investment coming in the form of spiritual growth in their kids.

"Outsourcing" is OK if you are aiming for good, but disastrous if you are aiming for godly. King David's life is a powerful reminder.

I wonder what David might have done differently in regards to his family if given another chance. If he had completed "The View From the Rocking Chair" exercise, would he have invested his life differently? ▪

CHAPTER NINE REVIEW & SMALL GROUP QUESTIONS

1. The statistic about young adults departing from their faith is sobering. What would you say is a primary factor in this phenomenon?

_____

_____

_____

_____

_____

_____

_____

2. Which of the "Six Differences" between good and godly have you observed most clearly?

_____

_____

_____

_____

_____

_____

_____

3. When you read about King David's family life, what do you find most surprising?

_____

_____

_____

_____

_____

_____

_____

4. What do you think are the most common reasons people "outsource" the spiritual training of their children?

_____

_____

_____

_____

_____

_____

5. What can be the negatives when a culture counts on the "professionals" to do the heavy lifting in terms of teaching our children about God and His ways?

_____

_____

_____

_____

_____

_____

CHAPTER TEN

CORE TRAINING
FOR GODLY

*Every father should remember that one day
his son will follow his example instead of his advice.*

— Charles Kettering

In the culmination of the film *Facing the Giants*, a small Christian high school football team long known for mediocrity finds itself trying to unseat the two-time defending state champs—a large public school with three times the number of players.

After a dismal start to the season and calls from parents for his termination, head coach, Grant Taylor, experiences an identity crisis that leads to a renovation of his core values. His change in heart spreads to a few key players and multiplies from there. As a result, a radically different football team takes the field for the final game.

Just as a transformed team could be traced to what happened at the core of the head coach, a transformed family can be traced to what happens at the core of the parents. With our understanding of the difference between good and godly in hand, let's consider what we must embrace at our core to aim for godly. There are two crucial elements that provide a necessary framework as we seek to do this.

PURSUE ONENESS

Malachi was called to preach a difficult message to God's people in a time when they were expecting accolades. If you drew a timeline from the reign of King David to the life of Christ, a span of about 1,000 years, Malachi would fall just past the midpoint.

Many of the Israelites had returned to Israel after their exile in Babylon. God had raised up Nehemiah to help them rebuild the walls of Jerusalem, and Ezra to help them restore the temple and many of the religious observances. God's people felt that the tide had turned in their favor and things were looking good in the Promised Land.

Malachi was selected to help God's people realize things were not as good as they seemed. Note how Malachi uses questions to engage the husbands and fathers:

> *And this second thing you do. You cover the Lord's altar with tears, with weeping and groaning because he no longer regards the offering or accepts it with favor from your hand. But you say, "Why does He not?"*

> *Because the Lord was witness between you and the wife of your youth, to whom you have been **faithless**, though she is your companion and your wife by covenant. Did He not make them one, with a portion of the Spirit in their union? And what was the one God seeking? **Godly offspring.** So guard yourselves in your spirit, and let none of you be **faithless** to the wife of your youth.* —Malachi 2:13-15, ESV

Malachi's charges the Israelite men with being "faithless" with their wives. The Hebrew word at the heart of the accusation is also translated "unfaithful," "breaking faith," and "dealing treacherously" and means separating from their spouse and their marriage covenant. In Malachi's indictment, we find two nuggets that are more valuable than gold.

First, if we are faithless with our spouse, we are also being faithless with God. How is this so? When we *abandon or move away from* our spouse, we are opposing God's plan for oneness in marriage. Oneness in marriage has been His design from the beginning: *"For this reason a man will leave his father and mother and be united to his wife and they **will become one flesh**."* —Genesis 2:24 We find this verse five times in the Bible! Jesus reinforces the point by quoting this same passage and adding: *"So they are **no longer two, but one.** Therefore what God has joined together, let man not separate."* —Matthew 19:6

Instead of moving deeper into God's plan for oneness, the Israelite men were moving in the opposite direction—abandoning their wives. We know God took the offense seriously in that He refused their offerings and acted as a witness against them. I can make this a history lesson or apply it to my own life. Being faithless with my wife—moving away from her instead of toward her—equals opposing God's plan, which equates to being faithless to God.

Before we go on, it is important to ask, "Why is oneness in marriage a critical part of God's plan?" Because oneness between the husband and wife accomplishes some of His greatest purposes—it is designed to:

- Reflect God's sacrificial love and forgiveness
- Refine our character so we become more like God
- Reveal God's glory and goodness [1]

When a husband and wife faithfully pursue oneness, the power of the gospel is brilliantly displayed. This display is meant to deeply influence our children.

Do you remember, from the Malachi passage, what God was seeking through the oneness of a husband and wife? *Godly offspring*—children who are increasingly like God and pursue what He cares about. Here we find the second priceless nugget. The state of our marriage—our faithfulness and oneness—profoundly affects the spiritual journey of our children. Being faithless with my spouse robs my children of the impact of seeing God's plan authentically lived out between their dad and mom. Being faithless with my spouse is the same as being faithless with my children.

If we want to aim for godly children, *we must aim for oneness with our spouse.*

When my wife and I reach a challenging spot in our marriage (yes, we encounter these), I am grateful for the driving force in Malachi's words. Faithfulness to my wife, my children, and my God means humbly, graciously, and steadfastly pursuing oneness with her. This is what my children need to see to grow to become more like God.

THE STATE OF OUR MARRIAGE PROFOUNDLY AFFECTS THE SPIRITUAL JOURNEY OF OUR CHILDREN.

Malachi's message brings a practical question to those who hope to have godly kids. ***"How are you pursuing oneness with your spouse?"***

Here are seven ways to pursue oneness that could be a good fit for your marriage. You might pick two or three to try and see how they benefit your relationship:

1. Sit on the couch and talk each night for thirty minutes after you put the kids to bed.

2. Go for a long walk and talk once each week.

3. Attend a marriage-building event once a year (e.g. marriage conference, getaway weekend).

4. Pray out loud for one another each morning before the kids wake up, or as you lie in bed together just before bedtime.

5. Schedule a standing date night, once or twice a month.

6. Read a book together, on the couch or in bed, a couple of times each week.

7. Stop everything to hug and kiss your spouse each day. Studies show it is healthy for children to see their parents show affection to one another. [2]

If you could incorporate just one of these seven activities into your lives, the one I recommend is sitting on the couch with your spouse every night once the kids are in bed (or in the morning before the kids wake up). I have seen this habit produce the biggest change in the "tone" of our marriage.

To make this time truly valuable, start by putting away the TV, computer, and cell phones. The goal is to give your eyes, ears, and mind all to your spouse for twenty to thirty minutes. This is a time to ask how the day went, laugh about things the kids did, and grow together as husband and wife.

For this to have maximum impact in our marriage, Chantal and I sit facing each other and I rub her feet while we talk. Researchers have found eye contact measurably affects our emotions, behavior, and ability to remember the content of a conversation. [3] Looking into each other's eyes as you communicate is more significant than you might think.

Call this idea "Nine O'clock on the Couch" and try it for a month. At that point, assess if your oneness has grown. If so, you are moving toward having godly children in one very substantial way.

PARENT GOD'S WAY

The ultimate passage on parenting in the Bible is called the *Shema* (sh-ma). This passage gets its name from the fact that *Shema* is the Hebrew word for "hear" which is the first word of the passage.

Moses wrote these words to the children of Israel after they had spent forty years in the desert and just before they were to cross into the Promised Land. God had Moses remind the Israelites of His plans for His chosen people one last time before they took possession of the land:

> *Hear, O Israel: The Lord our God, the Lord is one. Love the Lord your God with all your heart and with all your soul and with all your strength. These commandments that I give you today are to be upon your hearts. Impress them on your children. Talk about them when you sit at home and when you walk along the road, when you lie down and when you get up. Tie them as symbols on your hands and bind them on your foreheads. Write them on the doorframes of your houses and on your gates. —Deuteronomy 6:4-9*

This passage has long been one of the most revered texts in Judaism. The Jews immediately recognized its importance because it is God's prescription for transmitting the deepest values from generation to generation. In our modern thinking, it answers the question of how to create an entire family that loves and follows the Lord.

Many Orthodox Jews today still recite this passage three times a day. Many Jews stored a small copy of it in little boxes, called phylacteries, that they would tie on their heads and on their arms in an attempt to obey at least the letter of the law.

They would also put this passage in little boxes called mezuzahs that were placed at the doorframes of their houses. The nation of Israel took this passage very seriously.

Moses wrote these verses to parents. They were called on to do these things as leaders of their families. Just as you must prepare a foundation before you build a house, Moses first gives instructions to the parents about their own lives before he shifts the focus to how they should teach their children.

> *"Love the Lord your God with all your heart and with all your soul and with all your strength."*

The parents are exhorted to first live out their devotion to the Lord and commitment to His ways before they attempt to transfer this to their children.

> *"These commandments that I give you today are to be upon your hearts."*

Our children will know if we are not convinced about following God. We can fool many people but not those who live with us and watch how we live on a daily basis. Our efforts to teach them without first being convinced and committed ourselves will not produce results.

Once we have this foundation in place, we can focus on building a "godly" house.

> *"Impress them on your children."*

As a parent, you are given the unique opportunity to make a lifelong impression on the soul of your child. When you look at a coin, you observe a particular impression that will last for generations. Removing that impression takes a herculean effort.

God offers us, as parents, the chance to form a deep and lasting impression on our children of who God is and what He is like. How do we form this impression?

Through our example. The deepest impressions are made by our lives. We are always teaching our kids. Whether we like it or not, it is true. When our children watch us love the Lord with all our heart, soul, and strength, they learn how to do the same. As they watch our obedience to God, they can see what it looks like to have His commands upon our hearts. If they see us obeying God in some situations and disregarding His commands in others, they will powerfully learn that obedience to God (and other authorities) can be situational.

You have probably heard the saying, "More is caught than taught." Children consciously and subconsciously emulate the behavior of their parents.

On one occasion, I was wearing a long sleeve button down shirt on a day when my four-year-old son was wearing a similar shirt. I decided to roll up my sleeves and within two minutes, my son came over and said, "Dad, I can't get my sleeves up. Can you help me?"

Because children are designed to emulate their parents, God emphatically tells us that we must be the "real deal." To have kids that do not sit on the fence, with one foot in the world and one foot in church, we must get off the fence. If we want our kids to be "on fire for God," we must be on fire for Him.

Through our instruction. The second way we form a lasting godly impression on our children is through what we teach them.

> *"Talk about them when you sit at home and when you walk along the road, when you lie down and when you get up."*

Parents are not only called to be models for their children but also to serve as their primary instructors about God and His ways.

As we have already highlighted, many parents today feel they must delegate this aspect of training to "professionals." But in both the Old and New Testament, parents are given the calling and privilege of this role. [4]

Through our reminders of His truth. The final way to make a deep and lasting spiritual impression on our children is by providing continual reminders of God's truth.

> *"Tie them as symbols on your hands and bind them on your foreheads. Write them on the doorframes of your houses and on your gates."*

God has called parents to take action in keeping the truths about who God is and what He desires ever on our children's minds.

Consider how often your family would think about God's truth if you went through each day with a small box of Scripture tied to your foreheads and hands. Let us assume you did not stop noticing these adornments.

What would your thoughts be like if every doorway from one room to another read, "Be joyful always," or, "Pray continually," or, "Give thanks in all circumstances."

How would you respond if you saw, "I will never leave you nor forsake you" in huge letters on your garage door every time you pulled into the driveway?

God unveils a clear and consistent design in the Shema. We are to remember the truths about God and His ways at all times.

As we discussed earlier, God intends for people who trust in Him to become increasingly like Him. He makes us more like Himself by

151

renewing our minds so we think like He does. Reminders of God and His ways are an essential part of how we conform to be like our Creator.

THE "WHEN" OF THE SHEMA

We have addressed the question of how we impress our love for God onto our children from a strategic level. Now we will zoom in to the tactical, or more practical, level.

Our next key question as we look at the Shema is this: *When* are we to be making this impression on them? More specifically, *when* are we to teach them by our example, *when* are we to talk about the Lord and His ways, *when* are we to provide reminders of His truth?

God does not seem to be saying just ten minutes a day. We see a picture of parents instructing their children twenty-four/seven as they go about the day. What is the implied message to our children when we continually teach them about God and His ways? In some sense, it is proof that we genuinely believe what we are trying to teach them. We are willing to instruct them at every opportunity because it is so *important*. Conversely, when we do not constantly teach our children something we *claim* is of life or death importance, the silence is deafening!

THE GREATEST DISCIPLE-MAKER EVER

Who was the greatest disciple-maker ever to walk the face of the earth? I am guessing you will agree it was Jesus. How much time each day and each week did He think it would take to mold and shape true disciples—people who thought, spoke, and acted like He did?

The disciples had to leave their old lives to live with Jesus, to learn from Jesus, so they could become like Jesus. Jesus' call to "come and follow me" meant He would be making an impression on their lives twenty-four/seven. Nothing less would do for Jesus.

Should our approach to making disciples in our home be radically different? Obviously, we are not living in the same culture Jesus did. But, like Jesus with His disciples, we have our children around us twenty-four/seven. We have the chance to see all of life as an opportunity to mold and shape our children to become more like Jesus. If we choose to do so, we'll be following the example He set.

If you say "yes" to this call from the Lord to make disciples in your home as instructed in the Shema, who wins? If your children get to learn, by word and example, the most important things from the most important people in their lives, do they win?

If you take seriously the responsibility of teaching and reminding your children about the ways of God all through the day, what will happen in your life? Do you win also?

What about others who observe your family? If they get to see what it looks like for a family to faithfully follow Christ together, do they win?

And how will the Lord feel about all this? When we follow His plan, everyone wins. Everyone wins, as my kids remind me, "except the Devil."

IF YOU ARE DISCOURAGED AT THIS POINT . . .

As you read this chapter, you might be discouraged by what you see in the attitudes and choices of your children. You may feel some guilt because you have been operating off different blueprints than the ones we have studied. You may feel some shame at the fact that you are divorced and you have witnessed some of the scars in your kids' lives. If you are feeling something like this, can I show you a hopeful plan and promise?

Paul wrote to the Galatians because they were in a battle. Not a battle for their children, but a theological battle with false teachers. Many of the Galatians were battered and bruised. He closes the letter with these words:

> *"Do not be deceived: God cannot be mocked. A man reaps what he sows. The one who sows to please his sinful nature, from that nature will reap destruction; the one who sows to please the Spirit, from the Spirit will reap eternal life."*
> —Galatians 6:7-8

Paul does not sugar-coat the reality that the struggle goes on. But he provides a focal point, a step they can put into practice.

STEP ONE: Sow good seed—obey what the Lord has showed you.

In 1 Corinthians, Paul also uses the planting and harvesting metaphor and offers something crucial to remember in parenting. *"I planted the seed . . . but God made it grow."* —1 Corinthians 3:6 You cannot make your kids grow in the Lord; you can faithfully play your part.

STEP TWO: Remember, God produces the growth.

Paul finishes the previous section in Galatians with this promise from God. *"Let us not become weary in doing good, for at the proper time we will reap a harvest if we do not give up."* —Galatians 6:9 Weariness is part of every protracted battle and especially present in parenting. Paul declares that our perseverance will pay off.

STEP THREE: Don't give up!

The most powerful scene from *Facing the Giants* has the team captain, Brock, being challenged by the head coach to see how far he can carry a fellow player on his back while he does the bear crawl (known by the team as the "Death Crawl").

After the coach blindfolds Brock so he won't be limited by his own expectations, the captain makes his way down the field carrying his teammate while the coach shouts encouragement in his ear, "Don't quit! Don't quit! Don't quit!"

Propelled by the coach's nearness and passionate exhortation, Brock makes it the entire length of the field, finally collapsing in the end zone. When his blindfold is removed, Brock is astonished at what he has done. In that moment, he accepts the call to lead and grasps the value of wholehearted perseverance.

Brock's epiphany has a ripple effect among the rest of the team—an effect that ultimately leads them to the state championship.

God has given us a similar and unique calling in the lives of our children. Like the coach, He is right with us, providing the passion and encouragement we need to wholeheartedly persevere as we invest in the lives of those we will surely care about in the rocking chair.

If you realize you have been aiming for good and not godly, take heart! *It's never too late to begin* sowing the seeds of godliness into your family. The next chapter will offer some practical ways to accomplish that. ▪

CHAPTER TEN REVIEW & SMALL GROUP QUESTIONS

1. Why is the marriage relationship so significant to the spiritual health of children?

_____

_____

_____

_____

_____

_____

_____

2. The Shema (Deuteronomy 6:4-9) encourages us to make a deep impression on our children through example, instruction, and reminders of God's truth. Which of these is the easiest to accomplish? Which is the most difficult?

_____

_____

_____

_____

_____

_____

3. If we are to teach our kids throughout each day, what do we need to do this effectively?

_____

_____

_____

_____

_____

4. How would you compare the way Jesus made disciples to the ways we make disciples today?

_____

_____

_____

_____

_____

_____

_____

5. Consider parents you know who are examples of effectively teaching their children about God and His ways. What lessons have you have learned from them?

CHAPTER ELEVEN

_____

_____

_____

_____

_____

_____

_____

AIMING FOR GODLY

It is not the double reverse halfback pass that wins football games.
It is the effective execution of elementary ideas.

— E.E. Jennings

A few years ago, two thoughtful seminary-trained dads approached me on separate occasions with the same question: "What should daily life look like for my family if we are trying to follow the Lord?"

Since these conversations occurred within three months of each other, it highlighted the reality that strong biblical training does not make obvious the practical steps of aiming for godly as a family.

Which is more important—having the right mission and vision or taking practical steps that will help accomplish the mission and vision? The answer is both.

The mission and vision must be clear *and* we must take practical steps in the right direction. If something is not visible at the practical level, it is invisible. The practice of, or failure to practice, some of these everyday ideas will largely determine where you find yourself at the end of your life.

Here are a few ideas on how to aim for godly together as a family that our family has found to be effective. We have tested out many ideas that did not work out so well; we will not offer those. But the following suggestions have been effective and sustainable steps for us that I believe can also benefit your family. Think of them as our "Best Of" list.

1. STUDY THE BIBLE TOGETHER

The first idea to consider is regularly studying the Bible together - one verse a day. If the thought in the verse spills over to the next verse, study both verses that day. For historical books (e.g. Genesis, Nehemiah, Acts), we recommend a half chapter or chapter a day.

The idea is simple. Pick one book of the Bible and follow this pattern:

Review yesterday's verse.
Ask: "Who remembers last night's verse?"

Read today's verse.
Ask: "Who will read tonight's verse to us?"

Discuss the verse's meaning.
Ask: "Who has an idea what this verse means?"

Apply it to your lives.
Ask: "Who can think of a way to apply this in our family?"

Many of us want to be able to say we learned God's Word together as a family. But for virtually every family, the two biggest hurdles are: 1) finding time, and; 2) finding a good resource for family Bible study or devotional times.

The hurdle of finding time for family Bible study ends up being a values question. *Do we value this enough to make it part of our everyday schedule?*

Husband and wife must be in agreement to institute anything that is an everyday thing for a family. Making time for this has to be "on the calendar" for both Mom and Dad and will initially take some adjustments.

The best timing for most families is right before bedtime or right after dinner. The good news is that this incredibly valuable practice normally takes between five and thirty minutes a day.

> HUSBAND AND WIFE MUST BE IN AGREEMENT TO INSTITUTE ANYTHING THAT IS AN EVERYDAY THING FOR A FAMILY.

Finding the right resource may not be as difficult as you think. Many people shy away from using the Bible for family devotionals because it is intimidating and the parents do not feel qualified to teach and interpret it.

Purchasing a good study Bible and a trustworthy commentary (we provide recommendations in Appendix A) will go a long way to addressing the fear factor caused by certain obscure passages and provide helpful background information that is interesting to all ages.

Taking a cue from Chapter Five, in which we discussed the power and value of questions, asking questions is a solid approach and will help you see what your children are grasping and what still needs some review. As you consider the act of leading family devotions, remember there is no rocket science or Ph.D. required.

To graduate from seminary with a "Masters of Divinity," I had to be able to adequately defend the core beliefs of the Christian faith and articulate my statement of faith, reflecting the primary and secondary doctrines of the Bible. But after studying certain books of the Bible a verse each night with my family, I now feel I know these books two to three times better than when I graduated from seminary!

I have noticed our children grasping the background, context, and main message of each book we are studying. And it appears they are retaining this knowledge well beyond the time we study each book. This is largely due to the amount of time we spend soaking in these truths and the numerous opportunities they have to apply them to their lives.

Pray and ask the Lord to show you how you might take this step. Some of our most treasured (and funny) times come as we try to understand and apply God's Word as a family. For most parents, the choice to regularly read God's Word together is a practical one that will lead them one step closer to where they want to be when they reach the rocking chair.

At the end of a recent retreat, a young man who is a husband and father to a three-year-old said, "The idea that captured my thoughts more than anything else [during this retreat] was one day hearing my child say, 'I learned the Bible from my dad.'"

Of all the things we might want to hear from our kids when we are older, the grateful affirmation that we taught God's Word to them could inspire us to study and teach our families the Bible each day.

2. PRAY TOGETHER

Most Christians in America wish they spent more time in prayer. Some may feel an underlying guilt every time the topic of prayer is brought up. While an individual prayer life is important, what if you focused on growing your prayer life as a family?

Praying together deepens our relationships and grows our faith as we ask the Lord to move and watch His amazing answers. For some, praying together as a family may have bad connotations.

We've all experienced Dad's too-long prayer that could rival the President's State of the Union address or Mom's laundry list of her children's faults and entreaty for patience and perseverance. Prayer need not be everlasting or painful.

"Popcorn prayer," our family favorite, means everyone can pray a short prayer whenever they are ready. They can "pop" as many times as they would like while providing space for everyone to participate.

Choosing someone to open and close is helpful. Popcorn prayer contains two secret ingredients: brevity and volume. Prayers that are brief and loud enough for everyone to understand help each family member to stay engaged. Popcorn prayer can invigorate your family prayer life.

We have discussed how to pray. Here are some ideas about what to pray for as a family.

Pray for one another. In our family, sharing one prayer request each and having each family member pray for the next oldest or next youngest has helped us grow our hearts for each other.

Pray for people outside your family also, which develops compassion and an others-focus. Pray for extended family, friends, and neighbors who have not yet surrendered to the Lord.

> PRAY FOR PEOPLE OUTSIDE YOUR FAMILY, WHICH DEVELOPS COMPASSION AND AN OTHERS-FOCUS.

You may also pray for persecuted saints around the world and believers you know who are walking through difficult seasons. Pray for families who are considering divorce and children experiencing the pain of divorce.

My wife, Chantal, does a great job of making our children aware of prayer needs she discovers throughout the day. If she learns of one by phone or email, she will often gather our children to share the need at the appropriate level and then initiate "popcorn prayer." Afterward, they continue the school day or whatever else they are working on.

One of the greatest benefits of praying as a family is sharing the joy of seeing the Lord's answers to things we have prayed about.

I will never forget my daughters' reactions when they learned that a man, who we had long prayed for as a family, accepted Christ as his Savior.

When one of my daughters heard the news, she laughed and then began to weep tears of joy on my shoulder. The only thing better than watching God show His power and goodness is witnessing it together with those you love and have been praying with.

3. MEMORIZE GOD'S WORD TOGETHER

It seems the American church has embraced the idea that memorizing Scripture is a good idea . . . *for children*. For most adults, however, the thought of memorizing the Bible receives a less than enthusiastic reaction. Many adults think they are particularly "bad at memorizing verses."

Nowhere does the Bible indicate that Scripture memorization is for children only. In fact, the Bible provides plenty of evidence of Scripture memorization being part of a natural part of following Christ.

As an adult, Jesus regularly answered questions with Scripture from memory. He defeated Satan's temptation in the wilderness by quoting the book of Deuteronomy three times. Psalm 119 exhorts us eight separate times to meditate on God's words. And the letter to the Colossians encourages believers to let the word of Christ dwell in them richly.

As we saw in the previous chapter, the Shema in Deuteronomy 6 instructs us to keep God's commands in mind and in view like they were written on our head and hands. Because of this, many believers throughout history have adopted the practice of memorizing God's Word and testify that it has been a transforming practice.

One way your family can aim for godly is by selecting a passage of scripture to memorize together as a family. Pick a passage that is between forty and fifty verses in length so you can commit about one verse to memory each week and memorize the entire passage in one year.

ONE WAY YOUR FAMILY CAN AIM FOR GODLY IS BY SELECTING A PASSAGE OF SCRIPTURE TO MEMORIZE TOGETHER AS A FAMILY.

What passage should you memorize? Consider passages that, if you were stuck on a deserted island without your Bible, would help you faithfully follow Christ for the rest of your life.

There are so many tremendous passages to choose from but here are some of our favorites: Hebrews 11, Colossians 3, Romans 12, Matthew 5, 1 Peter 1-2, John 14, Titus 1-3, Philippians 1-4, Ephesians 6.

Pick a time each day, such as dinnertime, to review the verse you are working on that week. Once a week, try to say all the verses you have learned in your selected passage so far. Keep adding on verse by verse with the goal of finishing the chapter (or selected passage) by the end of the year.

One method we have discovered that dramatically increases our retention and makes the memorization process easier is setting the Scriptures to rhythm. We are in good company in adapting simple methods that help us remember God's Word. The Jewish people were known for putting Scripture to song so it could be more easily retained. Psalm 119 was created with twenty-two stanzas, each beginning with the next letter of the Hebrew alphabet.

We cooperate with God's design of the brain when we put Scripture to rhythm. You can listen to some examples at www.sonrisemountainranch.org.

We have adopted two traditions in our family that make this practice even more fun. We set the finish line for memorizing the entire passage at New Year's Eve and gather as a family that night to attempt to recite the complete passage from memory. Then, within the first week of January, we celebrate the completion of that year's passage with a special dinner at one of our family's favorite restaurants.

During the celebration, we give thanks to God for His help and provide a few clues to help the kids guess which passage we have selected for the next year.

When you are counting the cost of memorizing Scripture as a family, consider this: If your child begins memorizing a chapter of Scripture each year at age five and keeps up this practice throughout adulthood, what will be the result by the time he turns seventy-five?

Your son or daughter might sit in the rocking chair able to reflect and meditate on seventy chapters of Scripture! They may have also passed on this practice to their children and grandchildren. The living and active Word of God might be transforming generations. It could start with you.

4. SCHEDULE & HAVE FAMILY TIME EVERY DAY

Christ-following parents desire not just to have a good relationship with their children but to have a transforming relationship. We desire our lives to be used by God to transform our kids' lives. The lifeblood of transforming relationships is time together. Time together deepens trust. Trust is essential to transmit truth. Transmitting truth transforms our children.

Time Together → Builds Trust → Transmits Truth = Transformation

Spending time with others proves we consider them valuable. This is the tipping point of transformational relationships. You have heard the saying, "People don't care how much you know until they know how much you care." It is often quoted because it is often observed.

When we try to teach our children about God but are not willing to spend significant amounts of time with them, we undermine our own efforts. We talk of love but they do not perceive it.

With this in view, the next idea to consider in aiming for godly is to plan time every day to deepen relationships in your family members. From our observations, parking it in front of the television or computer each night will not accomplish this.

Watching a great family movie once a week *may* be ideal when you are filling the rest of your week with other relationship-building activities. Games are a great idea. Walks, wrestling, reading a book aloud, listening to radio theater, answering "Table Topics" questions on the couch—all of these can create feelings of closeness among family members.

Time spent together with the goal of growing relationships creates space for laughter and joy, two elements of family life that frequently disappear during a busy and hectic week.

> TIME SPENT TOGETHER WITH THE GOAL OF GROWING RELATIONSHIPS CREATES SPACE FOR LAUGHTER AND JOY.

In our family, if I tackle one of my kids on the couch, it is just a matter of time before everyone within earshot has joined the fray. Even our youngest, Vivian, will make a beeline toward the pile of bodies, though she frequently gets "bonked" during these episodes. No one wants to miss the tickling, laughing, and physical touch.

The time we spend wrestling or playing a game together directly impacts how our children engage during Bible study. They believe we care deeply about them, love to be with them, and so they listen carefully to what we teach them (on most days).

As with daily Bible study, scheduling is the long pole in the tent for this idea to become a reality. As families grow in number and children grow in age, scheduling time for everyone to be together becomes increasingly difficult. Parents who try to squeeze in family time **after** they put everything else on the calendar normally meet with failure.

Start with this question: *If time together is essential to transforming relationships, what is more important to us than time together as a family?* Then, make your family schedule reflect your answer. It may take some "deconstruction" of the family calendar. Keep asking yourself, *Is it worth it?*

5. SERVE TOGETHER

At one point in Jesus' ministry, the mother of two of his disciples approached Him and asked if He would give the place of honor to her sons when He "came into His kingdom." Afraid they would be short-changed, the other ten disciples expressed their dismay with the woman's attempt at a backroom deal.

The Master Teacher used this emotionally-charged moment to teach a penetrating truth:

> "*Whoever wants to become great among you must be your servant and whoever wants to be first must be your slave—just as the Son of Man did not come to be served, but to serve, and to give his life as a ransom for many.*"
> —Matthew 20:26-28

"Serving others" accurately describes Christ's life and should be able to describe His followers. Unfortunately, many Americans see "serving others" as something to be endured until we can get back to the fun stuff—recreation and entertainment. But our family has discovered this perspective can change radically through experience.

I have watched children, who previously dreamed of a trip to Disneyland, choose a family mission trip instead, after developing an appetite to serve. They experienced the joy, meaning, and even the difficulty of serving others for Christ and gained a new perspective.

It is our loss that many Christians and Christian organizations have accepted the notion that families with younger children can do very little to serve others either in local or foreign mission efforts. While putting a hammer in the hands of a four-year-old may not pass the practicality test, our experience strongly suggests that children enhance efforts to love and serve others.

Children break down cultural and socio-economic barriers like nothing else. When people see you bringing your young children to a foreign land (or different neighborhood) to serve, they *might* think you are crazy but they will believe you are safe. They are far more likely to engage you in conversation and receive what you have to offer.

Finish this sentence: "The best way to teach children to be others-oriented is to . . . " If your answer includes modeling an others-oriented life, your response reflects what we learned in Deuteronomy 6:6-7.

The Message paraphrase captures it nicely: *"Write these commandments that I've given you today on your hearts. Get them inside of you and then get them inside your children."*

If you want children who serve others, serve others with your children. Making a meal for neighbors, visiting and leading worship services at a nursing home, going on a mission trip—these experiences write the Lord's commands on our hearts and on the hearts of our children. Moreover, they yield a special joy when we do them together as a family. Chapter Fourteen will offer more ideas to help you ponder how you can regularly serve as a family in your current stage of life.

6. CREATE A CIRCLE OF ENCOURAGEMENT

Most of us hope to be able to look back on our key relationships and see they were founded on the love of Christ. One aspect of relationship with Christ is encouragement. God gives us encouragement throughout the Scriptures and exhorts us to "encourage one another and build each other up."

Something we've found to be a great way of doing this is the "Circle of Encouragement." Gather your family together in a circle so everyone can see each other. Have them share ways they have seen Christ working in or through other family members. The words must be authentic, but they can be short and sweet.

> "Eden, I saw Christ in you when you volunteered to play with your baby sister when she was fussy last night."

> "Mom, I felt God's love by the way you reacted to me when I dinged the car."

> "Maddison, it is beautiful the way you are putting your sisters' needs before your own."

Proverbs tells us, *"The tongue has the power of life and death."* —Proverbs 18:21 Nobody has to be taught how to use the tongue to harm others. But all of us need instruction, reminders, and God's help to unfailingly use our words to bring life. When a family practices genuine encouragement, it does not go unnoticed.

Once during a family conference on a mission trip to Romania, our family demonstrated the "Circle of Encouragement" for three to four minutes, sharing things we had noticed in each other during the trip up to that point. My first surprise occurred when the pastor who was translating got a lump in his throat. When we finished our demonstration, I was shocked to see half the people in the auditorium in tears. The Romanian families did not miss the beauty of a family sharing life and expressing love.

Realize that it may take a little while for your kids to get used to noticing the kind and loving acts of their family members, but it will catch on. Our experience shows that if you persist in this practice, one day you will see encouragement happening in your family spontaneously.

7. SING PSALMS, HYMNS, & SPIRITUAL SONGS AS A FAMILY

The next idea to consider is building in regular times in your family life where you are singing songs that point you to the Lord. Two times in the New Testament, followers of Christ are exhorted to *"sing psalms, hymns, and spiritual songs"* with one another (Colossians 3:16, Ephesians 5:19).

We sing one of these types of songs before meals, when we are driving in the car, when we are cleaning up after dinner and sometimes before or after our family Bible study. The phrase "psalms, hymns, and spiritual songs" is broad, so we take it to mean any song that helps us think about the Lord and His truth.

We sing some classic hymns ("Amazing Grace," "How Great Thou Art") and some praise choruses ("Awesome God," "Father I

Adore You"). We also listen to and sing along with Christian artists like Newsboys, Toby Mac, Chris Rice, Skillet, and Lecrae. (We have included a list of songs we enjoy singing in Appendix B.)

The directive to sing to the Lord appears to be for both the musically-inclined and the not-so-musically-inclined. Why might God have told all of His people to regularly sing songs about Him? If we think back to the Shema in Deuteronomy, we see God's plan for us to keep His truth in our minds throughout the day. What happens when you sing a song? Often, that song gets stuck in your head and you are singing (or humming) it for the next hour—or until it is replaced by something else.

God has designed us so that music can carry a message to us and through us in a unique way.

Neurologist Dr. Richard Pellegrino once declared in an interview, "Take it from a brain guy. In 25 years of working with the brain, I still cannot affect a person's state of mind the way one simple song can." [1]

I know a former professional football player who, for decades, refused to give up the ultimate control of his life to Christ. This tough and powerful man finally came to the point of surrender while listening to a woman simply and beautifully sing, "Jesus Loves Me."

Regularly singing godly music can remind us of God and His ways and help us become more like Him.

8. READ BOOKS ALOUD THAT HELP YOU THINK LIKE JESUS

Our family was driving through the Colorado mountains but in our minds we were all at the Czech border watching Brother Andrew attempt to take a car full of Bibles behind the Iron Curtain.

As the border guard approached, semi-automatic weapon in hand, to inspect the vehicle, Brother Andrew prayed, "Lord, you made blind eyes see. Now, would you make seeing eyes blind?"

That story, which we read aloud while on a road trip, shaped the faith of each one in our family and provided a treasured time we will not forget.

Living at this time in history, we have a couple thousand years of books from saints who have walked the path before us. "Listening" to these saints and their stories has great value. The value can be unlocked and experienced in our families when we read, or listen to, these books together.

Missionary stories in books like *God's Smuggler*, sermons, biographies, and allegories like *Pilgrim's Progress*, deepen our understanding of genuine faith, removing blind spots we may have from living in our modern-day culture.

Carving out one night a week to read a chapter in a compelling story could become a family favorite pastime (We have included a list of some of our favorite stories in Appendix C).

We have likewise enjoyed a number of stories recounted in dramatic audio productions. Audio theater has limited popularity today but was a mainstay for families in the mid-1900s. It may feel "old school" to gather around an iPod or CD player to listen to a story, but it provides a similar opportunity to discover eternal truths while you get lost in a story together. In addition, family road trips provide the perfect opportunity for this kind of activity.

9. TELL AND SHOW YOUR FAMILY EVERY DAY THAT YOU LOVE THEM

You have undoubtedly considered this idea before. However, many parents find their practice of this inconsistent. A crucial piece to aiming for godly is showing and telling your spouse and children every day that you love them . . . as if today is your last.

I do not know which day will be my last, but my hope is that, regardless of when it comes, all my loved ones will have no doubt about how I feel about them. One way to ensure that your spouse and children know you love them is by aiming to communicate it every single day.

Obviously, using words is an excellent way. Saying, "I love you," or "I'm so glad to be your dad," or "You are so precious to me" can brighten your child's countenance and clearly communicates love.

Hugs and other physical affection also convey love. Research indicates touch is a powerful thing.

Studies have shown simple touch boosts the immune system and negates the effects of stress. One study found the amount of touch babies receive can affect brain development by up to thirty percent. Dr. Jay Gordon, co-author of *Brighter Baby*, said, "Children who get a sustained form of touching, such as a long hug everyday are smarter." Studies strongly suggest we thrive when we regularly receive loving touch. [2]

> STUDIES HAVE SHOWN SIMPLE TOUCH BOOSTS THE IMMUNE SYSTEM AND NEGATES THE EFFECTS OF STRESS.

At this point, we should acknowledge that each person reading this book grew up in a different home environment. Some of us heard from our parents every day that they loved us while others had parents who assumed we knew how they felt. Some grew up getting a hug every day while others grew up in homes where there was very little physical touch.

Recognizing the type of home you grew up in sets the baseline for how you communicate with loved ones. At the same time, you are not confined to the mold of your parents. Follow the Lord in determining what you will be known for in this arena at the end of your life. You can be a very affectionate person even if you grew up in a home that expressed little affection.

THERMOMETER-BAROMETER

Our family uses something we call the "Thermometer-Barometer" as a means of expressing love and care. To do this activity, ask each person to give you two separate scores—from zero to ten—indicating their "thermometer" and "barometer" readings.

Your thermometer score is your "excitement about life" at this moment. Your barometer score is your pressure reading—how much pressure and stress you feel right now.

Each of my children tends toward a different reading. My third oldest daughter is Rebekah, and her Thermometer-Barometer score is usually an "eight/two." Her excitement for life is pretty high and her pressure level is fairly low. If those numbers suddenly change, I know something may be wrong in my daughter's life.

The Bible shows us a significant part of loving others in a Christ-like way is knowing their needs and attempting to meet them (1 John 3:16-18). Asking Rebekah her "Thermometer-Barometer" gives me the chance to understand not only how she is doing, but to also see if she has needs I can meet. This practice gives her evidence that I care how she feels and I desire to provide for her needs.

BLESSING YOUR CHILDREN

Finally, an idea that you may already have considered and practiced is showing your love for family by praying a blessing on them. For dads and husbands, this is one step to consider taking to provide spiritual leadership in your home.

For the past several years, I have had the privilege of ending every day by praying a short blessing over each of our children as they lay in their beds, just before they go to sleep.

Regardless of how well or poorly the day has gone, the last words they hear from their dad are a request for the Lord to bless them. My prayer is often something like this:

Father, thank You for Abby Grace. Thank You for the privilege of being her dad. Thank You for showing her that You are trustworthy. Lord, would You show her how precious she is to You and to me? Please give her Your peace as she sleeps tonight and pour out Your richest blessings on her life. Thank You for our relationship.

In Your Name, Amen.

Not long ago, I saw the power of this practice. A man who came on a retreat felt his relationship with his teenage daughter was shipwrecked and that it was having a detrimental effect on his marriage and his other children. During the retreat, he committed to ask God's blessing for his daughter each night. After he returned home, he sent these updates:

Day 1—*I prayed over my daughter tonight for the first time. I had been meaning to do this for days but something had obstructed this goal every night until this evening . . . I endeavor to continue this and make it a habit for both of us.*

Day 3—*Last night my daughter drove to her friend's house and forgot to call to tell us she had arrived safely. I texted, asking if she arrived safely. This was her response: "Yes, I'm going to bed now. Thank you for worrying about me! (:" Prior to [the retreat], she certainly would have responded with a nasty response.*

Day 93—This morning I was saying goodbye to each of my children with a kiss and a hug before reluctantly departing for a trip. In the past, my daughter would make herself scarce at these times. If I went to give her a hug, it was a one-way hug and it felt like hugging a dead fish.

This morning she not only stayed in the kitchen but initiated the hug—initiated it! Thank you, Lord. It wasn't the warmest of hugs, so her heart has more thawing to do, but there is hope. There are still wet towels on the bathroom floor and the bag of bread is open (a couple of Dad's pet peeves), but I have a daughter who believes I love her.

This practice can help our children believe they are deeply loved and precious to their parents and their Creator.

10. REMEMBER YOUR FAMILY "HIS-STORY"

In the book of Deuteronomy, God spoke through Moses to prepare His people to live faithfully in the Promised Land that they were about to enter. More than twenty times, Moses exhorted the people to remember and not to forget their God and how He had acted on their behalf. Remembering His faithfulness is a key to remaining faithful.

The last idea in this list is to find a way to remember your family "His-story."

Many years ago, my wife gave me a Christmas gift to help us carry this out. The gift was a special suede scrapbook with the title, "The McGee Family Record of God's Amazing Answers."

In it, she had recorded some of the obvious ways we had watched God move on our behalf up to that point in our marriage. Each page had a picture and a paragraph or two about how the Lord showed up. One page had our original prayer list of things that needed to happen when we left the Air Force and embarked on our time in seminary.

My faith is refreshed even now when I recount His answers to our prayers. Our children were too young (and some of them not yet born) to remember much about that transition. Yet, they have been able to read about God's faithfulness in that season and their faith has grown.

> MY FAITH IS REFRESHED EVEN NOW WHEN I RECOUNT HIS ANSWERS TO OUR PRAYERS.

Your family record need not be as elaborate as a scrapbook. We have friends who have placed special mementos on their living room mantle to memorialize the Lord's faithfulness to their family. They have a small toy car representing the Lord's protection during a major accident. Each token above the fireplace has a story and each person in the family knows how the Lord showed His goodness in that story.

Other families have used a special journal to record significant answers to prayers and unexpected ways the Lord has blessed them. The family adds to the journal at Thanksgiving or anytime they see the Lord's hand at work in a memorable way. As the journal grows, so does their faith and trust in their Heavenly Father.

However you choose to keep your family's "His-story," remembering the Lord's faithfulness is a rich and powerful intentional step that you will not regret in the rocking chair.

. . . .

In our culture, follow-through is at an all-time low. We have come to expect people to over-promise and under-deliver. Legal agreements are necessary in areas where people used to simply rely on one another's word.

Failing to follow through on the things that matter most should frighten us. Here are a few principles that will help you effectively implement the steps you have chosen to aim for godly:

PRACTICE TWO OR THREE AT A TIME

You might look at the list of ten practical steps and desire to begin eight new practices at once. How many will you achieve? Behavioral scientists have found the amount we bite off directly affects how much we actually swallow.

Franklin Covey studies suggest people trying to implement two or three new steps will be successful in two or three new steps. Those who try to incorporate four to ten new activities will succeed in only one to two of these. The ambitious (or delusional) who aim for eleven to twenty new practices, achieve, as you might have guessed, zero. [3]

Consider which of the ten practical steps you believe will be most significant for your family and choose two or three to implement. Exert maximum effort for three months, then take an assessment. If you have successfully incorporated these practices, consider adding others, keeping in mind that more is not always better.

UPHOLD YOUR ONENESS

In the previous chapter, we discussed the importance of oneness in marriage. We must keep oneness in view as we consider implementing these ideas. You can imagine the scene if one parent is encouraging the family to sit down for Bible study while the other parent is lobbying to watch television—not pretty at all.

If you are married, do not implement any of the ideas above unless both husband and wife support the decision. If only one spouse thinks it is best to take one of these steps, agree to pray together about it for a month and then see if anything has changed. The bottom line: Uphold your oneness and recognize it is an indispensable part of God's plan to shape godly children.

REMEMBER THE FLYWHEEL

A flywheel is a heavy round metal disc used in machinery. Great force is necessary to start rotating a flywheel, but very little force is necessary to keep it spinning.

You can expect to encounter the flywheel phenomenon when you implement any of these steps. Beginning a new practice to aim for godliness may meet resistance from our schedules, spiritual warfare, our children, and even our own will. Weeks or months of diligent effort may be required to put one of these ideas into practice.

Remember, it will not always be so hard. There will come a time when everyone is on board and even looks forward to it.

MAKE IT SUSTAINABLE

All of the ideas offered for your consideration are sustainable. If you set out to read the Bible in the next ninety days, you could finish it but would almost certainly not be able to repeat that feat in the next ninety days.

When you are selecting new practices to aim for godly as a family, choose ideas that you can begin, find a rhythm, and continue for the rest of your lives. Pick a frequency that marks a sustainable pace. The most impactful practices are those we make a natural part of our daily life.

SCHEDULE FIRST WHAT MATTERS MOST

Finally, I shamelessly repeat this principle from Chapter Eight because it is crucial. If you truly want to see some of these practices become a permanent part of your family's walk with God, put them on the schedule first. The only exceptions should be work and school if you do not have control over these.

Putting extracurricular commitments on the calendar ahead of these will drastically erode the likelihood that they will become a reality. Remember the words you hope to hear from your family in the rocking chair.

YOUR COMPASS CHECK

Now that the second question—Are we aiming for good or godly?—is fresh in your mind, we want to provide a chance for you to continue work on your Compass Check. Remember, this is your opportunity to take the truths that are most significant to you and to craft a tool to help you keep them in mind. You might find a review of your answers to the "Rocking Chair" exercise (page 27) helpful at this point. Don't forget to develop both "check-up" and "filter" questions.

Here's an example of a **check-up** question related to "good vs. godly":

Are we consistently taking the steps to be our children's primary teachers about God and His Word?

This is a **filter** question some people have found valuable:

Does this activity/book/movie/song bring us closer to God?

What question(s) can you ask yourself to see if you are on course in light of this question of "good vs. godly"? What question(s) will help you stay on course when new opportunities arise? What question(s) would help you hear the words you hope to hear as you sit in the rocking chair someday? Write your questions below.

_____

_____

_____

_____

_____

_____

_____

_____

_____

_____

We will review these questions when we finalize your Compass Check in Chapter Fifteen. ∎

CHAPTER ELEVEN REVIEW & SMALL GROUP QUESTIONS

1. What difference do you think it would make for you to regularly study the Bible together with your family (or loved ones)? What is the greatest obstacle to you doing this?

_____

_____

_____

_____

_____

_____

_____

_____

_____

2. When have you prayed with your family or a group of people for a specific request and seen a compelling answer from the Lord? What effect did that experience have on the relationships in the family/group?

_____

_____

_____

_____

_____

_____

_____

_____

_____

3. What is the effect on your family when you spend very little time together? How about when you spend regular time together, simply enjoying and cultivating your relationships?

_____

_____

_____

_____

_____

_____

_____

4. Which principle at the end of the chapter is most important to you as you consider new practical steps for your family?

_____

_____

_____

_____

_____

_____

5. Which one or two of the practical steps consistently lived out would have the greatest impact on your view from the rocking chair?

_____

_____

_____

_____

_____

_____

CHAPTER TWELVE

ARE WE AIMING FOR THE AMERICAN DREAM OR THE KINGDOM OF GOD?

I have learned the secret of being content in any and every situation, whether well fed or hungry, whether living in plenty or in want.

— The Apostle Paul

Who in America has it all?

Brad Pitt is not a bad answer. Good looks, *check*. Pitt has been voted the Sexiest Man Alive. A beautiful mate, *check*. Pitt has been married to or dated several beautiful actresses, including Jennifer Aniston and Angelina Jolie. Successful career, *check*. As an actor, Pitt has been nominated for multiple Academy and Golden Globe awards. Money, *check*. Pitt's net worth is estimated at greater than $150 million. [1]

What is it like when you have it all? Most people would like to know.

Pitt offered a glimpse into his life during an interview just prior to the release of one of his films:

Pitt: *Man, I know all these things are supposed to seem important to us—the car, the condo, our version of success— but if that's the case, why is the general feeling out there reflecting more impotence and isolation and desperation and loneliness? If you ask me, I say toss all this—we gotta find something else. Because all I know is that at this point in time, we are heading for a dead end, a numbing of the soul, a complete atrophy of the spiritual being. And I don't want that.*

Rolling Stone Magazine: *So if we're heading toward this kind of existential dead end in society, what do you think should happen?*

Pitt: *Hey, man, I don't have those answers yet. The emphasis now is on success and personal gain. [Pitt smiles] I'm sitting in it, and I'm telling you, that's not it. I'm the guy who's got everything. I know. But I'm telling you, once you've got everything, then you're just left with yourself. I've said it before and I'll say it again: it doesn't help you sleep any better, and you don't wake up any better because of it.* [2]

This is probably not the answer Americans would expect, but it is imperative for us to listen closely to his assessment.

The final question we will consider together relates to the issue of where we invest our time, our talent, and our treasure:

Are we aiming for the American Dream or the Kingdom of God?

Once again, we must define our terms:

The American Dream—a state of life focusing on financial security/independence, personal achievement for recognition, and the attainment of comfort and ease.

The Kingdom of God—the realm of God's rule and reign; where the Lord's will is done.

Before we go farther in our discussion of the American Dream, I need to make clear what we are *not* saying.

My wife and I both love our country and served in the U.S. Air Force. We were willing to fight and die to defend and protect America. We are deeply grateful for the privilege of living in the United States. It is of the greatest importance that this honest look at the American Dream not be misperceived as a diatribe against the United States. Our hope is that this book will serve as a blessing to Americans.

THE REDEFINED AMERICAN DREAM

The American Dream of today is different than the American Dream of the early 1900s. In the first half of the 20th century, the American Dream represented the opportunity for any person to work hard and reap the benefits without the systemic constraints that had been the norm in Europe for centuries.

In theory, America offered a life without a class system, without racism, and without religious persecution. The reality was that these general influences were significantly muted in the United States in comparison with most other countries on the planet. The dream of "equal opportunity" was much closer than it had been before.

The content of the American Dream has gradually morphed

during the last third of the 20th century and the first decade of the 21st century. The advertising industry has contributed much in this transformation. We can watch the advertisements to understand more of what "we" are seeking. What picture is painted for our destination?

WE CAN WATCH THE ADVERTISEMENTS TO UNDERSTAND MORE OF WHAT "WE" ARE SEEKING.

You have the regal-looking older gentleman walking on a white sand beach. You might think he is in his late-fifties since he has some gray hair but notice he also has "six-pack" abs.

Beside the man we see his wife or girlfriend. Likewise, her age is a little unclear. She has the body of a thirty-something but looks like she might be the gentleman's original wife. We will call her "Miss Everywoman." She adores her man and her enviable life. He is the picture of contentment.

Off in the distance, we glimpse their yacht anchored just off shore. They have no needs and give the appearance of true peace. The message of the ad is simple. If you work hard and make the right investments, this could be you when you retire. Getting "set up" for our retirement years is a key element of the new American Dream.

Another picture illustrates what might happen if we do not faithfully pursue the American Dream. This commercial invites us into the life of an older couple, facing the strain of medical bills that come with declining health. They are sitting at a kitchen table strewn with bills and financial statements. They have just come to the realization that their nest egg has run out. They look at each other with deep distress. *What will they do now?*

They are well past their prime. Maybe Walmart has an opening as a greeter. Will they end up homeless?

Investment firms convey the message that there is a specific number—a goal for your investment portfolio. If you reach this number, you are assured of the golden years of retirement. If you fail to achieve this number, all bets are off. Your fears of working at Walmart until you die and homelessness are not unfounded.

The encouraged response to these two alternatives is to be like the ant and not the grasshopper. Work hard, store up for later.

Aesop's fable contrasts these two bugs and assigns honor to the ant that forsakes pleasure now so he will have enough food when the winter comes. The lazy grasshopper desires only to play and sing and has no eye on the coming change of seasons. When the snow comes, the grasshopper finds himself starving, and makes a plea to the ant whom has an abundance. The ant shakes his head as he turns his back on the grasshopper's request.

Aesop's fable is timeless and generally accepted as the way things should be. This parable helps us grasp the thinking of the updated American Dream. As we consider the larger question of this chapter, we should note two aspects of this story.

First, Aesop presents only two categories—there are ants and there are grasshoppers. Diligence describes those who save up for themselves; laziness is a fair title for those who end up in financial need. While this aspect makes the fable clear and applicable to everyone, we need to determine if that is an accurate assessment biblically.

Second, the *Ant and the Grasshopper* touches on a universal fear: Will I end up running out of what I need to live?

Abraham Maslow, one of the most influential psychologists of the 20th century, identified this as the most significant in the hierarchy of needs. Self-preservation is a deep-seated, powerful motivational force that we will build our lives around unless there is something higher in view.

THE DREAM REVEALED

Our previous picture of Mr. Contentment and Miss Everywoman on the beach contains an additional ingredient of the American Dream that may be more visible to those from other cultures.

An African bishop was invited to speak at numerous churches throughout the United States. After talking with hundreds of American Christians and observing our culture, he remarked, *"America has been taken captive by the spirit of comfort and ease."*

The American Dream of today elevates the pursuit of these two elements. Hard equals bad and something to avoid if possible; easy equals good and desirable. The retirement years only appear attractive if they are characterized by comfort and ease.

Once again, the ad campaigns prove helpful as they hold up a mirror to see what we desire.

Office products giant, Staples, has made their primary selling point that they provide you with an "easy button" for life. They even sell an easy button which declares, "That was easy," when you press it.

I came across an ad in an airline magazine claiming that with their machine, I could get a full body workout *in four minutes a day*. Not to be outdone, another company offers a fabric belt for your midsection that effortlessly produces "ripped" abdominals while you go about your day. The pursuit of "something for nothing" (or almost nothing) still lives today.

Parents with several children regularly experience a negative reaction when they share the news of another child on the way. Instead of excitement and joy, they meet concern and angst. When you dig down below the surface, you find the reaction springs from the belief that additional children will make life harder, not to mention threaten your 401K.

The American Dream does not prohibit applause for everything that is hard. The hard years of medical school and residency are admired because a high paying job awaits on the other end. Swimming two hours in the morning before school and two hours after school is praiseworthy, because the honor and prestige of making the Olympics is a worthy payoff.

Doing hard things can be part of the American Dream . . . *if* they produce the appropriate personal gain. Herein we find the last stream of the underlying current that all Americans encounter.

The new American Dream values personal achievement that brings recognition. Whether they are willing to talk about it or not, most Americans desire to be well-known.

Half of young adults recently responded that their generation's top or second-most-important life goal is being famous. [3]

The term "famous" might be a little strong for some, but few Americans will deny they desire to be noticed and recognized as distinctive. Bumper stickers tout the accomplishments of our children. Christmas cards read much like a résumé, listing off the litany of endeavors and accomplishments from the past year. Few of us, if any, are immune to the craving to be noticed.

> HALF OF YOUNG ADULTS RECENTLY RESPONDED THAT THEIR GENERATION'S TOP OR SECOND-MOST-IMPORTANT LIFE GOAL IS BEING FAMOUS.

And the American landscape has proved to be fertile soil for making personal recognition a high value. Jake Halpern, author of *Fame Junkies,* remarked, "Fame is an equal opportunity tantalizer." [4] Reality TV shows and YouTube have planted the seed that going from anonymity to stardom is possible for anyone.

Personal blog pages and Facebook have allowed everyone to achieve celebrity status at some level.

Imagine the reaction if I transported someone from 100 years ago to sit with me in front of a computer where I pulled up the

Facebook page I had created for them and informed them this page could be viewed by billions of people around the globe. Undoubtedly, they would be wondering what they had done during their lifetime to warrant such attention.

This attitude toward individual recognition does not pervade every culture. One of my Romanian friends acknowledged the contrast between his culture and ours. He said, "Americans want to stand out from the crowd. In Romania, we have a saying that the head that stands above the rest of the crowd will be chopped off." The American fascination with fame is not unknown in other parts of the world but it is not universal.

Counselors and psychologists have begun to wonder about the effects of the American passion for fame, primarily evidenced in the meteoric rise of Facebook.

Kit Yarrow, a psychologist at Golden Gate University, has expressed her concern about young people choosing to present themselves on the Web versus the intimacy that comes with real communication. "My fear is not so much for our society but for a sense of emptiness and depression these kids might have as they age," she says. "They're putting their resources and energy and validation and self-worth into what people who aren't close to them think of them, which is fame." [5]

An abundance of material possessions, comfort, ease, and some level of celebrity—these ingredients swirled together make for a powerful cocktail called the American Dream that has become the drink of choice today. Like most cocktails, too many sips can dramatically affect our thinking, the way we walk, and our direction in life.

With the American Dream adequately defined, let us turn our attention to one of Jesus' favorite topics.

THE KINGDOM OF GOD

If you asked most Americans about the primary message of Jesus during His earthly ministry, their answers might include some of the following:

Love
Forgiveness
The Golden Rule
Heaven and Hell
Eternal Life

Few would identify "the Kingdom of God" as one of His primary messages. But it was.

If we comb the gospels, we find Jesus mentioning the Kingdom of God 103 times. Many of the parables start out, "The Kingdom of Heaven is like . . . " Jesus regularly said the Kingdom of God (or Kingdom of Heaven) "has come near," is "at hand," and "has come upon you."

He sent out the twelve and then the seventy-two disciples to heal the sick and preach this message: "The Kingdom of Heaven has come near to you."

The Kingdom of God is the content of the good news (Matthew 9:35). The Kingdom of God is what we are to pray will come to earth (Matthew 6:10). The Kingdom of God is what we are to seek first above and beyond other pursuits (Matthew 6:33).

Jesus summarized His mission with these words, *"I must proclaim the good news of the kingdom of God . . . because that is why I was sent."* —Luke 4:43

Dr. Ian Howard Marshall formerly served as the President of the British New Testament Society and is Professor Emeritus of New Testament Exegesis at University of Aberdeen in Scotland. Quite a mouthful. In addition to his titles, he looks like, sounds like, and is a Bible scholar.

Marshall noted, "During the past sixteen years I can recollect only two occasions on which I have heard sermons specifically devoted to the theme of the Kingdom of God [. . .] I find this silence rather surprising because it is universally agreed by New Testament scholars that the central theme of the teaching of Jesus was the Kingdom of God." [6]

If we think this theme will fade in importance, we do well to remember what will be written on Jesus' thigh and robe when He comes again on a white horse—*"King of Kings and Lord of Lords."* —Revelation 19:16

With the prominence of this message in view, we can briefly revisit the two definitions from the beginning of this chapter.

The realm of God's rule and reign. What are the elements of a kingdom? To have a kingdom, you need a king, subjects of the king, and the territory where the king is recognized as ruler. Many lives have turned on a dime in simply recognizing this—there is a King and you are not Him! Faithful subjects in a kingdom embrace the king's will and seek to live by his values. The territory of the Kingdom of God is the choices, relationships, thoughts, words, and actions that acknowledge the Kingship of God.

Where the Lord's will is done. The Lord's Prayer gives us a captivating glimpse into the Kingdom of God. In this model for prayer, we are taught to ask our Father for His Kingdom to come to earth just like it is in Heaven. "Your Kingdom come, Your will be done." The coming of His Kingdom is inexorably linked to His will being done.

We are invited to imagine what it is like in Heaven when the King of Heaven makes a decree. The inhabitants of Heaven do not yawn or act like they did not hear the King. They do not respond with a half-hearted nod. They do not pull out their whiteboards and make a list of "pros and cons" for doing the King's will. When the King makes His will known, the reaction of all those in Heaven is enthusiastic affirmation, delight, and worship of the King.

For those involved in carrying out His will, there is immediate and wholehearted obedience. Amazingly, we are exhorted to pray for this scene to happen here on earth, in our lives, today. When we live affirming God's authority in our lives, we live inside the Kingdom of God and we can honestly describe it as heaven on earth—or "on earth as it is in heaven."

Hopefully, the discussion of these terms has highlighted the radical difference between the pursuit of the American Dream and the pursuit of the Kingdom of God.

WHO IS WINNING

If you are not sure who is winning the battle in the hearts of people—the American Dream or the Kingdom of God—consider these statistics:

Eighty-one percent of 18- to 25-year-olds surveyed in a 2006 Pew Research Center poll said getting rich is their generation's number one or number two life goal; 51 percent said the same about being famous. Only 10 percent said becoming more spiritual was in their "top 2." [7]

In an annual survey of college freshmen by the Higher Education Research Institute at the University of California-Los Angeles, 2005 data shows that money is much more on their minds than in the past. The percentage who say it is "essential" or "very important" to be "very well off financially" almost doubled from 1967 to 2005, rising from 42 percent in 1967 to 75 percent in 2005. During the same period, "developing a meaningful philosophy of life" dropped in importance by almost half from 86 percent to 45 percent. [8]

THE AMERICAN DREAM VERSUS THE KINGDOM OF GOD

We can evaluate these two paths in a variety of ways, but ultimately, the most convincing appraisal comes from those who can give us a first-hand account of each option. So we continue our assessment of the American Dream versus the Kingdom of God by listening to those who have walked the talk.

WHAT DOES THE AMERICAN DREAM DELIVER?

We have already considered Brad Pitt's perspective. In a similar fashion, Billy Joel has reached dazzling heights in terms of the American Dream. Money, fame, the beautiful girl—he can speak from experience.

Fresh out of rehab, Billy Joel says he's looking for someone to spend his life with and plans to rent an apartment in Manhattan to meet women. "I'm not going to meet anyone out here," said Joel who lives in East Hampton, a posh community on nearby Long Island.

"The happiest times in my life were when my relationships were going well—when I was in love with someone and someone was loving me. But in my whole life, I haven't met the person I can sustain a relationship with yet [...] I'm angry with myself. I have regrets."

Joel, who is divorced from model Christie Brinkley, will continue touring this fall with Elton John, and Twyla Tharp will take to Broadway a play called "Movin' Out," featuring modern dance interpretations of Joel's songs. But the rocker said his success—including a place in the Rock and Roll Hall of Fame—is of little consolation.

"You don't get hugged by the Rock and Roll Hall of Fame, and you don't have children with the Rock and Roll Hall of Fame," Joel, 53, told The New York Times Magazine. "I want what everybody else wants; to love and to be loved and to have a family." [9]

I grew up listening to Billy Joel and envied his position when he married arguably the most beautiful model of the 1980s. This evaluation of his life would not be believable except that it came from his own mouth. His statements, like Pitt's, begin to renovate our vision for what the American Dream, in all its glory, actually produces.

Don Hewitt was the long-time executive producer of *60 Minutes*, one of the most popular television news magazines ever created. Hewitt was interviewed at age 81, during the rocking chair timeframe in his life:

Hewitt strode into his office and gestured toward the walls. There hung photographs of presidents, diplomats, foreign leaders and entertainers. There were notes from Presidents Reagan and Eisenhower. A constellation of Emmy awards. Arrays of plaques, posters, and medallions. "I'm not trying to be an egomaniacal maniac, but look," he said, "I don't want to lower the temperature. Where do you go? What do you do that's going to be like this? What I've got to do is feed my soul." [10]

Hewitt, in his own words, produces a CAT scan of his soul. His achievements and renown have failed to satisfy the longings in his soul and bring him peace. Bewildered, he searches for the destination that can provide true contentment.

Hewitt's comments, when added to Pitt's and Joel's, force us to this question, "How much of the American Dream is enough to satisfy?" How much fame, money, and comfort will bring contentment?

Among the key elements of the American Dream, wealth appears to be the lure that has the most chasing after it. Many believe that once they possess great riches, happiness and contentment will follow. So we look to those who have obtained almost unthinkable amounts of money to speak to this issue.

John D. Rockefeller was the first American billionaire and often considered the richest person in history, when inflation is taken into account. Rockefeller remarked, "I have made many millions, but they have brought me no happiness."

William Henry Vanderbilt, when he died in 1881, was the richest man on earth. His testimony sounds much like Rockefeller. "The care of $200 million is enough to kill anyone. There is no pleasure in it."

And finally, we consider the straightforward words of John Jacob Astor, who was the first multi-millionaire in the United States and the 4th richest man in U.S. history, "I am the most miserable man on earth." [11]

Those who have drunk deeply of the American Dream provide a consistent testimony. If the jury is still out in your mind, listen to the One who claimed to be the source of Living Water. ∎

CHAPTER TWELVE REVIEW & SMALL GROUP QUESTIONS

1. To what degree has the Body of Christ been influenced by the "American Dream" (as we have defined it)?

_____

_____

_____

_____

_____

_____

2. Why do you believe Jesus' message about the Kingdom of God has not been well-received today?

_____

_____

_____

_____

_____

_____

3. Which of the six quotes from those who have lived the American Dream is most striking to you? Why?

_____

_____

_____

_____

_____

_____

4. Why do you believe many Christians in America feel so influenced by the pull of the American Dream?

_____

_____

_____

_____

_____

_____

_____

5. We have asked and answered this question: How much of the American Dream is enough to satisfy? What is the most effective way to present this question to our children (and the younger generation) for their careful consideration?

_____

_____

_____

_____

_____

_____

_____

CHAPTER THIRTEEN

INVESTING IN
THE KINGDOM

Only a life lived for others is worth living.

— Albert Einstein

Jesus spoke often on this topic but a handful of selected passages allow us to capture the essence of his message. Notice how He speaks to the struggle we have when contemplating what will bring contentment. These passages have great value if we allow them, once and for all, to settle this question in our heart.

> *"Therefore I tell you, do not worry about your life, what you will eat or drink; or about your body, what you will wear. Is not life more important than food, and the body more important than clothes?...So do not worry, saying, 'What shall we eat?' or 'What shall we drink?' or 'What shall we wear?' For the pagans run after all these things, and your heavenly Father knows that you need them. But seek first*

his kingdom and his righteousness, and all these things will
be given to you as well." —Matthew 6:25, 31-33

Those who follow Christ are meant to pursue different things than those who do not call God their Father. If God is your Father, you are meant to focus on His business, the Kingdom of God, while resting in His promise to take care of your business or needs.

"No servant can serve two masters. Either he will hate the
one and love the other, or he will be devoted to the one and
despise the other. You cannot serve both God and Money."
—Luke 16:13

You must choose between the pursuit of God and the pursuit of money. From Jesus' standpoint, pursuing both or sitting on the fence is not possible. We are meant to see money as an instrument to serve God and His purposes.

"Watch out! Be on your guard against all kinds of greed;
a man's life does not consist in the abundance of his
possessions." And he told them this parable: "The ground
of a certain rich man produced a good crop. He thought to
himself, 'What shall I do? I have no place to store my crops.'
Then he said, 'This is what I'll do. I will tear down my barns
and build bigger ones, and there I will store all my grain
and my goods. And I'll say to myself, 'You have plenty of
good things laid up for many years. Take life easy; eat, drink
and be merry.' But God said to him, 'You fool! This very
night your life will be demanded from you. Then who will

get what you have prepared for yourself?' This is how it will be with anyone who stores up things for himself but is not rich toward God." —Luke 12:15-21

Your personal "net worth" is not the sum of all that you own. Those with the most toys do not win in God's eyes. Storing up wealth for yourself so you can "take life easy" and "be happy" is ultimately a foolish and fruitless pursuit.

"Do not store up for yourselves treasures on earth, where moth and rust destroy, and where thieves break in and steal. But store up for yourselves treasures in heaven, where moth and rust do not destroy, and where thieves do not break in and steal. For where your treasure is, there your heart will be also." —Matthew 6:19-21

From an eternal perspective, storing up what is treasured on earth is laboring in vain. When we invest in the things that are treasured in Heaven, our investments will be valuable for all eternity. What you treasure will be proven by your choices.

It is remarkable how well Jesus captured the ethos of the new American Dream. As in so many encounters recorded in the gospels, Jesus looks into the depths of our souls and invites us to believe that investing our lives in what He cares about is the only path to contentment. His message turns the American Dream on its head.

Out of His love, he gives us warning, encouragement, and promise—coming at this crucial topic from every angle so the truth is clear. Out of His love, He removes our blindness so we see that seeking the Kingdom and seeking the American Dream are diametrically opposed.

THE GREATEST THREAT TO THOSE AIMING FOR THE KINGDOM OF GOD

The Bible declares Solomon was *"wiser than any other man."* —1 Kings 4:31 Like his father, Solomon is a crucial study for parents who want to lead their children to follow God. Put mildly, Solomon was a paradox. He experienced some of the highest heights and descended to unspeakable depths.

Most Christians remember Solomon as a generally positive role model. We remember Solomon was chosen by God to build the temple in Jerusalem. We compliment others by saying they have the "wisdom of Solomon." Even Jesus uses Solomon's clothes and world-famous wisdom as a foil to make His point. But we miss the most precious point of Solomon's life if we go no farther than the positive aspects of his character.

God gave Solomon *"a breadth of understanding as measureless as the sand on the seashore."* —1 Kings 4:29 But despite this boundless understanding, Solomon directly disobeyed God in taking foreign wives. With his unparalleled wisdom, Solomon constructed places of worship for other gods—places that could be used for child sacrifice. It is fair to call Solomon the wisest *and* most foolish man of all.

Solomon experienced what I call "spiritual hypoxia." Hypoxia is a medical term describing a lack of oxygen to the brain. When someone experiences hypoxia, they may have a variety of symptoms without being able to recognize what is happening.

The term is significant in aviation because it can be a silent killer. If a pilot experiences the initial stages of hypoxia and does nothing about it, he or she may eventually pass out. Landing an airplane is pretty difficult if you are unconscious.

In the early stages of hypoxia, a pilot might notice tingling lips or hands, a mild dizziness, or a slight change in the colors they see. In the next stage, they might experience a lack of coordination, muscle fatigue, or a feeling of euphoria. If the hypoxia continues, the pilot will suffer poor judgment, a lack of awareness, and loss of consciousness as the brain is starved of oxygen.

Solomon's hypoxia was rooted in this one mistake: He adopted the affections of his culture. Even after dramatic encounters with God and tremendous blessings, Solomon began to love what the world around him loved. He began to value what his culture valued.

The symptoms of his spiritual hypoxia were his desire for women, fame, and material things—the pleasures of this world. He never noticed the initial symptoms of his spiritual hypoxia. I imagine it would have been exceptionally difficult for anyone to notice, when the whole world was idolizing your wisdom.

The symptoms became increasingly visible as the number of wives and chariots grew, but Solomon stayed the destructive course. When he began building the first place of worship for another god, Solomon had lost consciousness, spiritually speaking.

What I'm about to say is the most important point of this chapter. Spiritual hypoxia—the initially faint yet gradually deepening love of the things of the world and adoption of our culture's values—*is the greatest threat* to those aiming for the Kingdom of God. Spiritual hypoxia has insidiously shipwrecked the lives of countless people.

> SPIRITUAL HYPOXIA IS THE GREATEST THREAT TO THOSE AIMING FOR THE KINGDOM OF GOD.

If someone is suffering from spiritual hypoxia, they are likely to brush off the diagnosis. The teenager who has changed her listening habits from Christian music to Katy Perry will scoff when their parents show concern.

One brutal fact for parents is that moms and dads often open the door to spiritual hypoxia. Their loss of awareness in a particular area can lead their children into dangerous territory.

Ironically, Solomon's father, David, wrote the words that contained the cure for his son's malady. *"Your love is better than life . . . My soul will be satisfied [in You] as with the richest of foods."* —Psalm 63:3,5

If Solomon had taken these words to heart, his life—along with the life of his son Rehoboam, and the destiny of the nation of Israel— would have been vastly different. Rehoboam, who was the next king, completely turned away from God and, consequently, the nation of Israel was divided into two separate kingdoms during his reign.

No doubt Solomon had plenty of people around him admiring his palace, his women, and his horses. They all looked good. But I wonder if one of his counselors ever asked him what he treasured most?

Solomon became unconscious to his purpose. Israel was meant to be a lighthouse to the world, showing all the other nations what God was like. The people of Israel needed a godly leader to shepherd them in the ways of God. Solomon's eyes came off of God and others and rested on himself—his own desires and pleasures.

Solomon is believed to have penned the book of Ecclesiastes. In it, he discloses that he withheld no pleasure from himself—yet found all that he pursued to be meaningless. The man who had the pleasures of the world at his disposal failed in his search for purpose, contentment, and lasting joy.

NO ONE IS IMMUNE FROM THE THREAT OF DRIFTING OFF COURSE AND TAKING HIS FAMILY WITH HIM.

After reading about Solomon, it is apparent that no one is immune from the threat of drifting off course and taking his family with him. Jesus often said, *"He who has ears, let him hear."* We, too, should listen carefully and not forget.

KINGDOM MATH

Jesus presents a type of math that does not work well in the classroom or with a financial planner. Yet it is a math that helps unlock the mystery of true contentment and joy.

1 – 0 = 0

"For whoever wants to save his life will lose it . . . What good will it be for a man if he gains the whole world, yet forfeits his soul?" —Matthew 16:25-26

Our unwillingness to lose our old lives—the life where we are "in charge," where we get to call the shots, and where the primary beneficiary of our lives is ourselves—keeps us from the life God intends us to have.

We cannot retain the old life and experience the new. The entry point to the new life is the death, or complete surrender, of the old.

1 – 1 = MANY

" . . . but whoever loses his life for me will find it.
—Matthew 16:25

"I tell you the truth, unless a kernel of wheat falls to the ground and dies, it remains only a single seed. But if it dies, it produces many seeds." —John 12:24

The surrender of our old lives to follow Jesus opens up an entire kingdom and universe of opportunities where our lives are used to eternally impact not just one other person, but many.

He will not fail to use your life to change the lives of others if you put your life under His control and direction. He will use your life in ways that are beyond what you can ask or imagine. This is no imposition on Him—it is what He created you for. When He stands at the door and knocks, this is exactly what He has in mind when He comes in as the King of your life.

What we invest our lives in ultimately comes down to an issue of trust. When Jesus says, "Whoever wants to save His life will lose it but whoever loses his life for me will find it," we can either believe what He says or not. When He promises to provide what we need when we seek His Kingdom first, we can either trust Him or not. It is valuable to be honest with yourself about your level of trust in the words of Jesus. Do you trust Him?

A LIFE "FOR ME" OR "FOR OTHERS"

Consider the goal of your actions when living for the American Dream versus living for the Kingdom of God. Who is the primary recipient of the benefits? You can sum up the distinction between the two lifestyles like this—a life "for me" or a life "for others."

Jesus makes the trajectory of life simple for those who would follow Him through His own example. *"For even the Son of Man did not come to be served, but to serve, and to give His life as a ransom for many."* —Mark 10:45

Ponder the statements of Jesus we have reviewed in this chapter. So what happens when Christians pursue the American Dream instead of the Kingdom of God? Put another way, if our new DNA as Christ-followers contains the code to live for others but we operate against these blueprints and live for self, what would be the effect? We might expect something like the modern day assessment of theologian and author Dallas Willard that many Christians lead lives of quiet desperation. [1]

Jesus' words forecast to us across the ages that we should plan to experience despair, frustration, and misery if we continue to live for ourselves. God allows this fruit so we might see and believe living for others is the ultimate way of life.

In the early days of the Salvation Army, founder William Booth desired at Christmas to send out a message of encouragement to Salvation Army missionaries serving around the world. As the story goes, money was scarce and the cost of a telegram was based on how many words the telegram contained. Booth sent a one-word message to inspire the troops—"Others."

There is good evidence that those serving with the Salvation Army embraced Booth's message. In May 1914, a freight ship named the "Empress of Ireland" sank with 130 Salvation Army staff on board. Sadly, 109 of the 130 drowned but not one of the 109 that perished was found with a life preserver.

Survivors from the accident told how the Salvationists, as they were called, took off their own preservers and strapped them on others saying, "I can die better than you can." [2]

Since Booth's Christmas telegram, "Others" has been the motto of the Salvation Army and is a fitting motto for those who would seek first the Kingdom of God.

WHAT GREATER CALL IS THERE?

The call to introduce others to their Creator, Father, Savior, and Guide and to help them become like Him is unmatched in its importance. The call to rescue people from the control and influence of Satan so they can live gloriously under the kingship of God is unparalleled. Jesus proclaimed His mission, prophetically spoken about Him 700 years earlier by the prophet Isaiah:

*"The Spirit of the Lord is on me, because he has anointed me
to preach good news to the poor. He has sent me to proclaim
freedom for the prisoners and recovery of sight for the blind,
to release the oppressed, to proclaim the year of the Lord's
favor."* —Luke 4:18-19

The call for followers of Jesus to seek first the Kingdom of God
is the call to live out this mission out of love for Him and love for
others. What are we doing that is more important than preaching the
good news to the poor, proclaiming freedom for those imprisoned
by the Devil, restoring sight to those who are blinded to God's love
and purposes, releasing those living in oppression, and announcing
the limited-time invitation into God's grace?

We have been rescued to go rescue others. How could we come
to see this calling as commonplace and secondary to the callings
from the world around us? For so many of us, this greatest calling
has been watered down to a paltry, poor-tasting medicine instead
of the living water it is intended to be. May we never believe, and
may our children never see us believe, that this is anything but the
greatest and highest calling on our lives.

In the next chapter, we will look at practical ways to answer the
call and aim for the Kingdom of God. ∎

CHAPTER THIRTEEN REVIEW & SMALL GROUP QUESTIONS

1. Which of Jesus' quotes from the beginning of this chapter do you believe is the best critique on the American Dream?

_____

_____

_____

_____

_____

_____

2. When have you personally witnessed spiritual hypoxia affect a friend or family member?

_____

_____

_____

_____

_____

_____

3. Has there been a season of life where you felt the effects of spiritual hypoxia? What were the symptoms and how did you combat it?

_____

_____

_____

_____

_____

_____

4. In light of our presentation of "Kingdom Math," whose example has increased your faith that the Lord will powerfully use a surrendered life to impact others?

_____

_____

_____

_____

_____

_____

5. Why do we often not perceive Jesus' calling to "set the captives free" as the greatest calling on our lives?

_____

_____

_____

_____

_____

_____

CHAPTER FOURTEEN

AIMING FOR THE KINGDOM OF GOD

The happiest people are those who do the most for others.
The most miserable are those who do the least.

— Booker T. Washington

After Jesus' crucifixion and resurrection, He made the most of His remaining time on earth. He continued to prepare His followers for the mission He was leaving them to accomplish. We find this mission in Acts 1:3:

> *"After his suffering, He showed himself to these men* [the disciples] *and gave many convincing proofs that he was alive. He appeared to them over a period of forty days and spoke about the Kingdom of God."*

Jesus spent time making sure His disciples believed in His resurrection and grasped the work He wanted them to do.

Just before His return to heaven, He gave them this charge:

"Go and make disciples of all nations, baptizing them in the name of the Father and of the Son and of the Holy Spirit, and teaching them to obey everything I have commanded you. And surely I am with you always, to the very end of the age." —Matthew 28:19-20

The King of Kings made His will clear for His people. He did not ask them to figure out what their mission should be. He left them (and us) a clearly defined mission of incomparable importance.

So often, what is not clear to us is the vision of how we can participate in making disciples and expanding His Kingdom. Our mission is straightforward; the vision, not so much.

Yet this vision is crucial. Leadership books over the past fifty years repeatedly echo the biblical message about the importance of vision. Proverbs 29:18 tells us: *"Where there is no vision, the people perish."* (KJV) The Hebrew word for *perish* can be literally translated to mean, "cast off restraint."

Many leadership resources are quick to highlight the reality that people will not continue to play their parts if they cannot see the how their roles contribute to the greater victory. Every one of us needs vision to play our part.

OUR KIDS LEARN TO BE "FOR OTHERS" BY WATCHING US BE "FOR OTHERS."

As parents, we deeply desire to see the beauty of our children living for others and not the ugliness of them living for themselves. As we have considered in previous chapters, our kids learn to be "for others" by watching us be "for others." Our lives as parents are intended to provide vision that compels our children, over time, to make similar choices.

As children see God use their parents to change lives and expand His kingdom, they gradually develop an appetite to live for others.

If we want children who live for the Kingdom, we can be the vision they need. "Be the change you want to see" was Gandhi's famous expression that reflects these biblical truths.

The following practical ways of aiming for the Kingdom of God are intended to provide vision for you and your family. These ideas can be undertaken by families with children as well as couples who do not have children. These ideas are just a few of the things you can do as a family to seek God's Kingdom, but we hope they will allow God to develop vision in you.

THREE CIRCLES

Where do we start when thinking about aiming for the Kingdom of God? In Acts 1:8, Jesus tells His disciples, *"You will be my witnesses in Jerusalem, and in all Judea and Samaria, and to the ends of the earth."*

His followers were told to impact their world starting with those closest to them and stretching to the ends of the earth. The Kingdom of God is meant to expand from the inside out—from inside our hearts to those closest to us, to our neighbors, to our community, and to the whole world. We have found thinking about three concentric circles, from closest to farthest, is a helpful model.

INVESTING IN THE KINGDOM OF GOD IN YOUR NEIGHBORHOOD

In terms of relationships in America, there is still something special about living in the same neighborhood. Certainly it's not exactly the same as fifty years ago, but a noteworthy connection remains for those who live in the same neighborhood.

You can still ask your neighbors for a cup of sugar or invite them to join you for a meal, while you would never drive across town and ask someone to do the same without some other connection point. This relational bond opens the door for some unique opportunities to expand the Kingdom.

1. PREPARE A MEAL FOR A FAMILY IN NEED

While this idea seems incredibly obvious, we may sometimes omit the elements that make it the most meaningful. Allowing our children to help prepare a meal is not the easiest, and may double the amount of clean-up necessary, but it can provide a readily accessible opportunity to serve others together as a family.

To make this idea even more meaningful, pray as a family before you deliver the meal, have your children prepare a homemade card, and deliver the meal together as a family.

2. DO SOMETHING KIND FOR AN UNBELIEVING NEIGHBOR

The idea of performing "random acts of kindness" has found its way into movies, T-shirts, and bumper stickers. For Christ-followers, our acts of kindness would not really qualify as random. We are acting out of God's love poured into our lives as we pour it into the lives of others. "Unexpected" might be a better term than "random."

Brainstorm as a family what you might be able to do in the next month to show God's love to your neighbors. Mowing their lawns, shoveling snow from their driveways, taking them cookies, raking their leaves—these acts of service are normally received with gratitude. You may want to ask permission for ideas like washing someone's car or weeding flower beds. You may even want to do some research to surprise them with their favorite drink or treat from Starbucks. Combining these acts with prayer can enhance the effectiveness and meaning for everyone involved.

3. HOST A BARBEQUE

In most neighborhoods today, the norm of contact between neighbors is waving to one another as you pull into your garages. We might say hello to them when we see them outside doing yard work or on a walk, but most of us experience a shallow relationship with our neighbors.

How could we create a little depth of relationship that God might use to expand His Kingdom? Hosting a barbeque or "block party" for one other family or multiple neighborhood families is one viable way.

You may feel that to be intentional in expanding the Kingdom of God you must hand out a gospel tract as your neighbors arrive or host an impromptu showing of "The Jesus Film" after dinner. But intentional does not mean awkward—it means purposeful.

Before the barbeque, talk as a family about the goal of showing God's love and pray He will use the time. Go into the event with eyes open to the opportunities the Lord may provide to go deeper with your neighbors.

Get to know your neighbors as you share a meal. Listen well. Asking God's blessing on the meal might be the only time you mention the Lord. After the event, continue praying for your neighbors and looking for more opportunities to bless them.

Inviting your neighbors over for a dinner might be the first step in cultivating a rich relationship that God uses to deepen another family's faith or to reveal Himself to them for the first time.

4. HOST A SIX-WEEK MARRIAGE OR PARENTING STUDY

OK—this one may feel a little more challenging but it is a great next step for some who have tried the previous ideas. Host a study to help your neighbors with a felt need—marriage or parenting. To get something like this started, you might call some of your neighbors or stop by their houses and use a script like this:

> "Hi, we are the McGees and we live just around the block. Our daughter Eden rides the bus with your daughter Kelsey. How are you doing today? In a few weeks we will hosting a six-week video-based study about marriage. It will be humorous, leave time for some discussion, and is Christian-based. We think our time together will be fun and might help make our marriages stronger.
>
> We will host the study at our home on Thursday nights from seven to eight thirty, starting on October fourth and ending November eighth. We'll have dessert and coffee for about thirty minutes followed by a thirty-minute video and thirty minutes of discussion.
>
> We are inviting some couples from the neighborhood and would love for you to join us. Our older kids [or babysitter] will play games and help watch any kids who come so you are welcome to bring your children. Even if you can't make all the sessions, it would be great to have you there."

While attempting something like this may be out of your comfort zone, it is a great way to reach out to your neighbors. Most adults are humbled at some level by the challenge of marriage and parenting. These topics provide some common ground that can be the starting point for some very meaningful conversations.

Is there a risk in doing this? Yes. They may call you "Jesus freaks" as soon as they close the door, even for something as simple as this. They may talk to other neighbors about you. But they will know you are interested in getting to know them and will know that you believe in God.

Even if those you invite do not attend, there are still benefits. If the couple who received this invitation is facing divorce six months later and has nobody to turn to for help, they may remember your offer and come to you for help.

Do you want to be known by your neighbors as a family they could turn to in their time of need? We've included a list of resources in Appendix A if you are interested in trying this idea.

What part can our kids play in something like this? They can be friends to any other kids who attend, even helping supervise if they are old enough. As a family, we can pray before and after each session for God to expand His territory. Together, we can help make dessert and prepare the house for the arrival of guests. Our children can learn what it looks like to reach out to our neighbors.

INVESTING IN THE KINGDOM IN YOUR COMMUNITY

Investing in others in your community often requires a higher degree of planning than ministry to your neighbors. The upside of ministry in this larger circle is a greater number and variety of opportunities.

1. FIND A NURSING HOME

The most forgotten generation in America today are the elderly who are waiting out their time in nursing homes. Hour after hour, day after day, year after year they sit. Many receive regular visits from family members. Others receive visitors once or twice a year. Some never receive a personal visit.

There are few smiles and many smells in a nursing home. This is the perfect setting to show God's love and care to some of the neediest individuals in our society. Simply find a nursing home in your community and begin to visit the residents regularly.

Most nursing homes and assisted living facilities conduct worship services. Many times they do not have enough churches or groups to lead these services. Your family could commit to lead a worship service one time each month—singing a few songs, leading a ten- to fifteen-minute devotional, and then talking and praying with those who attend. Or volunteer with a church providing these services.

This has been one of the more valuable experiences for our family during the last few years. And eloquent sermons and beautiful harmonies are not required in this venue. All that is needed is your presence, God's love, a willingness to listen, share, and pray. Anyone can do this.

The smiles I see when we arrive with our six kids are inspiring. The "thank you's" and tears from the residents put a lump in my throat and recalibrate my perspective.

Your family may also enjoy visiting on holidays or delivering Christmas gifts in December. Opportunities abound and residents are not the only ones affected. We have seen nursing home staff start attending church and even pray to receive Christ as Lord.

2. PRAY FOR AND REACH OUT TO FAMILIES ON YOUR CHILD'S ATHLETIC TEAM

If your child plays a sport, consider your involvement in this pursuit as an opportunity to bring God's Kingdom to others on the team. If you are going to invest the time, make the most of it and be intentional.

Before the season begins, circle up as a family and consider all the ways you can build meaningful relationships, serve others, and share Christ's love in the context of your child's participation on that team. Select two or three of the best ideas you come up with and put them on your family schedule. Pray together regularly that the Lord will use these steps to take new ground.

We know a family whose teenager ran track so they invited all the kids on the high school track team to attend church with them followed by a barbeque and volleyball at their house. Ten kids, most of whom did not regularly attend church, came and developed a tie to that family that the Lord used in visible ways throughout the rest of the season.

Getting to know those you interact with throughout the season also allows them to see what a family who loves the Lord looks like. With so many broken homes today, do not underestimate the opportunity to "tell" others about God in the simple example of a loving marriage or a dad nurturing his daughter.

3. CAROLING FOR THE KINGDOM

I did not grow up in a musical family. We had someone show up once at our house singing Christmas carols when I was a teenager, and to this day, I still remember the intense embarrassment I felt.

All this to say, I share this idea against my natural inclination. But how often can you show up at someone's house as a family, ring their doorbell, and begin to sing about Christ the Lord? I have been amazed, year after year, at how the Lord has used a handful of families singing about God to bless others and change lives.

Here are a few tips we have found helpful if you want to use caroling as a community outreach:

- Consider going with a few other families.
- Strategically select the families you plan to visit.

- Consider taking along a plate of cookies for each family you visit.

- Reserve five to ten minutes after caroling to connect with those you are caroling to.

We are not surprised anymore when a mom or dad tears up, or when caroling leads to more meaningful conversations, or when someone finally accepts an invitation to attend church.

A few years ago, we asked if we could carol in our local Starbucks, where we know some of the staff. One of the families we carol with owns an old school bus that we used to transport all the carolers, so our arrival at Starbucks did not go unnoticed.

Six days after that evening, we received this note (the names have been changed):

Hi,

This is in appreciation for the wonderful group of carolers at Starbucks last week. Things have been really tough for my family lately. My wife was laid off (though she is working now) and we lost our house to foreclosure and were forced into bankruptcy. It has been extremely difficult on our family and our marriage. The joy had completely gone out of my life. I am a Christian but have been pretty disconnected lately. Starbucks is my one guilty pleasure.

We pulled into the parking lot on Tuesday the fourteenth and I saw your school bus with everyone getting off and heading into Starbucks. I immediately went into self-centered mode thinking, "Great, now I have to wait in line behind thirty people for my flipping cup of coffee." I jumped out of the car before my wife even got it parked so I could beat you all inside to order. I hustled past everyone at the door and whispered to Cindy to start my drink before everyone ordered. All of a sudden you all started singing.

I couldn't believe how self-absorbed I had been and how rude I was to cut in front of all of you. Your singing was beautiful and it came from a place of pure joy. Then to top things off, you bought my drink for me. I want to tell you that in that instant, in that moment in time, you made a difference in my life. God reached out to me and said, "Bryce, I'm still here, I still love you and I forgive you for being so self-centered." I want to thank you from the bottom of my heart and I pray that God continues to richly bless you all this Christmas season and always.

Merry Christmas in Christ,

Bryce Michaels

I would not believe this account if I had not personally seen it happen. Stories like this challenge us to leave our comfort zones to see the Lord use our families to expand His Kingdom.

We circle up as a team and pray before, sometimes during, and after the caroling. At the end of the evening, we enjoy hot chocolate together. It is one of the highlights of our Christmas season.

4. VOLUNTEER ONCE A MONTH AT A SOUP KITCHEN, PREGNANCY CENTER OR HOME FOR SINGLE MOMS

Virtually every community has a church or para-church ministry effectively serving and sharing Christ with the needy. Most of these ministries welcome volunteers and allow families to serve together if the parents are present to supervise.

The relationships you'll create are more important than the tasks you'll accomplish. Regular participation creates relationships with the ministry staff and those you are serving. These relationships are the avenues God uses to expand His rule and reign and bring the joy of serving others.

5. CONSIDER FOSTER CARE

One of the most beautiful expressions of the heart of God I have ever seen has been watching a husband and wife welcome an abandoned child into their home with no strings attached. Foster care is an amazing pathway to advance the Kingdom of God in the lives of those who have had little opportunity to experience His goodness.

We have been encouraged in recent years in watching an increasing number of God's people say "yes" to this opportunity to change lives. You can learn more about foster care from your state foster care specialists.

INVESTING IN THE KINGDOM AROUND THE WORLD

God has created us to have a heart like His—a heart of compassion for people all over the earth. Jesus commanded us to make disciples of all nations and be His witnesses to the ends of the earth.

Expanding the Kingdom around the world typically requires partnership with others already investing in foreign ministry efforts. Watching God at work around the globe expands our understanding of His mission and helps us grasp the enormity of God.

While some have made the ideas of foreign missions and

sharing Christ with your neighbors an "either/or," but going back to Acts 1:8, the most faithful picture of God develops when we see home and abroad as a "both/and."

1. GO ON A MISSION TRIP

When I was in seminary, my wife and I decided it was time to go share Christ's love and make disciples beyond the city where we lived. We searched for short-term mission trip opportunities where we could take our four children and minister as a family.

International Family Missions was one of the only organizations at that time that would take us. We traveled to Juarez, Mexico, with six other families and our lives changed forever.

On the bus ride home, my wife and I agreed we would go on trips like these for the rest of our lives. Little did we know where that small course correction would take us in the years to come.

Family mission trips have changed the way our family thinks, talks, and prays on a daily basis. We believe God is continually at work all over the planet because we have seen it. Virtually every day, we discuss mission trip memories or things we have learned on our trips because we have had rich experiences that deeply impacted us.

FAMILY MISSION TRIPS HAVE CHANGED THE WAY OUR FAMILY THINKS, TALKS, AND PRAYS.

Our prayers regularly reach around the globe because we have believing and non-believing friends in faraway places. From the youngest to the oldest, we are different because we have had these opportunities. We are grateful for the difference.

Many organizations now offer short-term mission opportunities for families. (Appendix D has a list of these organizations, including Sonrise Mountain Ranch, and a list of suggested steps to move ahead with this idea.)

An international mission trip is no small undertaking but it can provide the kind of transformational experience for a family that changes what everyday life looks like. These words came from a 14-year-old who went on a family mission trip:

When I first heard I was going to Romania I was not too thrilled. I had my first soccer tournament that weekend and just really did not want to go. I was angry that I might lose my position on the team and thought the trip would be a waste of time.

After getting to Romania, things started to change. The trip changed my perspective on how God does work around the world. I met some amazing people and shared some truly amazing experiences with them. I left the country with a totally new attitude from how I started. I wouldn't have traded the trip for the world.

Stories like this make a family mission trip worth considering.

2. JOIN WITH OTHER MINISTRIES REACHING OUT ALL OVER THE WORLD

Compassion International and Food for the Hungry effectively minister to the physical and spiritual needs of children and adults throughout the world. Both of these ministries have programs where your family can provide financial support for a child or a family while developing a relationship with them through correspondence.

Many local churches have ongoing partnerships with missionaries and ministries serving around the world. Gather information about these ministries, discuss and pray together about the opportunities, and select one to partner with through prayer and financial assistance.

3. CONSIDER ADOPTION

There are approximately 132 million orphans on the planet today. [1] Like foster care, adoption is a stunning demonstration of the heart of God that forever changes the adopted and the family that adopts.

Adoption, local or international, is a decision worthy of research and contemplation. Our journey alongside friends who have adopted has given us a healthy respect for the inherent challenges, as well as the greatest admiration for those who embrace them. At the end of the day, adoption is an undeniable way to bring the Kingdom of God to a child in need and represent the Father who has adopted us into His family. Focus on the Family has a number of great resources for those interested in finding out more.

DUE DILIGENCE BEFORE YOU INVEST

Since we mentioned the idea of partnership several times in this section, there is one important note to add. Before you partner with a local church, ministry, or missionary, or invest your resources, be sure to do some research.

The Bible strongly encourages us to examine the character, mission, and vision of the ministry leaders we join. Plenty of Christians have failed to take this step and regretted it for a long time afterward.

In many aspects of our lives, we clearly see the need to build a level of trust in relationships before we move ahead. Few people will select a contractor to build their house without looking closely at the contractor's track record.

Similarly, before you partner with a ministry, do some research, discuss your findings, and pray for clarity from the Lord. This groundwork will provide a greater opportunity for a deeper, long-lasting relationship to develop. When you find the right fit, we encourage you to jump in with both feet and watch the Lord use your family in ways better than you could have planned.

WATCHING OTHERS

One of the greatest motivators to live for others and seek first the Kingdom of God has been watching friends humbly and faithfully walk the path before us. Their stories fan into flame our desire to take the next step.

Some friends of ours are approaching retirement age. Their two children are both in college and they are in a good place financially. They love to travel and long envisioned this next season as their time to see the world. They have always been Kingdom-minded and had a startling revelation when their two children first left the home.

The King helped them see He had more plans to use their lives to imprint kids with His love. They are now in the process of adopting three teenage siblings who have been living at an orphanage in Mexico for 10 years. This couple knows their lives are not their own and are joyfully looking at the next season of making disciples through parenting.

My father was a successful college and pro football player before his career as a college football coach and athletic director. Throughout his career, he was always "in demand." Walking around a football stadium with my dad before a big game always made me feel important.

Every twenty or thirty seconds, someone in the crowd would

greet him, "Hello, Dr. McGee" or "Good job, Coach McGee." The stadium security would immediately recognize him, so every door was opened for us and no boundaries existed as we walked from the locker room to the field to the press box.

During my dad's career, he was always with the important people. He sought the trophies and treasures of the American Dream. Toward the end of his career, he surrendered his life to Christ, telling each of his four kids that he had chased the "brass ring" offered by the world and that what he obtained never brought fulfillment.

OUT OF HIS FAITH, HE SHOWED LOVE TO THE "LEAST IMPORTANT" PEOPLE.

When my dad retired, his status gradually changed. The number of phone calls and the amount of recognition dropped substantially. In that time, I watched his values change as well. I saw my dad begin to spend time each week with meth addicts in a modified rehab program.

Instead of talking regularly with the best-known football coaches in the country, conference commissioners, and sportswriters, my dad invested time in the "fools" and "hopeless" of society—those who had repeatedly chosen a drug that would destroy their mental abilities, careers, and families. Out of his faith, he showed love to the "least important" people. This example, even from late in his life, has made a mark on his children and grandchildren.

Another family we know has four sports-loving boys. They have made the decision to let their kids play on one or two teams each year. When they are in the midst of baseball season, they spend a lot of time at the ball field and at fast food restaurants. If you watch them for ten minutes at either place, you can tell they are seeking first the Kingdom as a family.

When they are at a practice or game, they are continually reaching out to other families on the team. They serve the coach and team, encourage each of the players, and make connections with the dads and moms in attendance. The parents listen well, invite people to church, laugh often, invite people out to dinner, and pray with people whenever they get the chance. Their kids play hard, serve others, laugh a lot, and are very respectful to their parents.

This family has a few restaurants they frequent more than others. When you walk into one of these restaurants with them, you would think they owned the place. It is common for the manager to greet them by name and the person standing behind the counter to have a few minutes of conversation with them. Frequently, employees will come say hello when the family has been seated and even give the mom a hug.

If they are at a sit-down restaurant, they regularly address their server after they have learned his or her name, "We are just about to pray before our meal. Is there anything we can pray or do for you?"

You might have a hard time believing the conversations that come from this question. This family simply loves people wherever they go and they have Kingdom relationships to prove it.

> MANY PEOPLE WILL *SAY* THEIR RICHES ARE FROM THE LORD. NOT AS MANY TAKE THE EXCESS AND INVEST IT TO CHANGE THE WORLD.

Some other friends of ours have been blessed with great wisdom and business acumen and have acquired significant wealth through the exercise of these gifts. In conversation, they do not hesitate to note that all they have is the Lord's.

Many people will *say* their riches are from the Lord. Not as many take the excess and invest it to change the world.

But because this couple has lived with open hands, the world is different, in clear and compelling ways. The blind have received their sight, the hungry have been fed, places of worship have been built, the message of Christ has been preached, and marriages have been saved through the resources, leadership, and encouragement of this family. As Jesus exhorted, they have been "rich towards God" and the Kingdom has advanced.

YOUR COMPASS CHECK

Now that the third question—Am I aiming for the American Dream or the Kingdom of God?—is fresh in your mind, we want to provide one last chance for you to work on your Compass Check before we finalize it in the next chapter. Since it has been a while, you might find this is a valuable time to review your answers to the "Rocking Chair" exercise (page 27). Don't forget to think about both "check-up" and "filter" questions.

Here's an example of a **check-up** question related to "the American Dream or the Kingdom of God":

If we look at our calendar and checkbook, what have we been seeking first?

Some people have found this to be an effective **filter** question:

Would doing this lead us more toward the American Dream or the Kingdom of God?

What question(s) can you ask yourself to see if you are on course in light of this question of "The American Dream vs. The Kingdom of God"? What question(s) will help you stay on course when new opportunities arise? What question(s) would be helpful in light of things that have pulled you off course in the past? Remember, this is brainstorming. Write your questions below.

_____

_____

_____

_____

_____

_____

_____

_____

_____

_____

Now it is time to finalize your Compass Check. ■

CHAPTER FOURTEEN REVIEW & SMALL GROUP QUESTIONS

1. What are the greatest barriers to your investing in the Kingdom?

_____

_____

_____

_____

_____

_____

_____

2. On a scale of 1 to 10, how do you rate your current relationships with your neighbors? What would be a great next step to grow those relationships for the Kingdom?

_____

_____

_____

_____

_____

_____

_____

3. When have you observed or experienced the impact of a mission trip? What was the most significant change in yourself? In others?

_____

_____

_____

_____

_____

_____

_____

4. Have you seriously considered foster care or adoption? What are your thoughts?

_____

_____

_____

_____

_____

_____

5. Of all the ideas and stories in this chapter, which one sounds best for your family?

_____

_____

_____

_____

_____

_____

CHAPTER FIFTEEN

THE COMPASS CHECK

Don't come down here and cry about it; go home and live it!

— A.W. Tozer

On September 1st, 1983, a Korean Airlines (KAL) 747, carrying 269 people, took off from Anchorage, Alaska headed for Seoul, Korea. Shortly after takeoff, the aircraft began to deviate from the planned route of flight by the equivalent of two degrees. After almost an hour of flight, KAL Flight 007 was 12 miles off course. Limited radar coverage over the northern pacific prohibited ground controllers from identifying this error. The pilots for KAL 007 believed the autopilot had them on the correct flight path and did not discover the ever-increasing deviation from course.

Ninety minutes into the flight, the deviation was 60 miles. After three hours, the jumbo jet was 160 miles off course. When it mistakenly overflew Russia's Kamchatka Peninsula, Soviet fighter jets were scrambled, believing the intruder to be an American military reconnaissance aircraft. As the unsuspecting airliner continued its incursion into Russian airspace, a Soviet Su-15 maneuvered into position and fired two missiles. The crippled aircraft crashed into the sea twelve minutes later, killing everyone onboard. [1]

This sobering story brings a sharp point to some of the principles we have discussed in previous chapters. First, navigation is of life or death importance, so it deserves our focused attention. Information from the cockpit voice recorder revealed the pilots of KAL Flight 007 had *no idea* they were off course or that they faced grave danger. When the missiles exploded at the tail end of their aircraft, they were dumbfounded. [2]

Second, accepting only a general sense of the direction we are headed can lead you on a path toward a destination you will regret. KAL Flight 007 looked good from a distance—it was generally headed in the right direction. It was never off course more than 10 degrees in the more than five hours of flight before it was shot down. However, the pilots did not closely inspect their navigational instruments to determine if they were truly on course.

Third, it is vital to recognize the threats we face. The pilots did not recognize that a flight path deviation could result in destruction by a lurking adversary. If they had a clear understanding of the threat, then their actions—and the outcome of the flight—would have been different. Our situation is remarkably similar. The apostle Peter helps us see clearly, *"Be alert and of sober mind. Your enemy the devil prowls around like a roaring lion looking for someone to devour."* —1 Peter 5:8

The valuable reminders from this tragic account provide additional motivation to take our last step of finalizing the means to check our compass. Up to this point, you have contemplated life as a journey and clarified the vision for your destination at the end. You have considered the importance of navigation and the significance of determining what you will use as your compass for life. You have grappled with the significance of your choices and the part they play in leading to your destination. You have been presented questions that you will find important at the end of your life: Are you aiming for busy or full, good or godly, the American dream or Kingdom of God?

In answering these questions, you have had the chance to check your compass, to see where you are headed and if course corrections are needed. Our last step then, is to develop a fully functional way to check your compass for the rest of your life.

COMPLETING YOUR COMPASS CHECK

You have been introduced to the Compass Check—a tool to help you make choices each day with key biblical truths and your desired destination in mind. This is your opportunity to complete your personal or family Compass Check and learn to utilize this tool to its greatest value.

In both navigation and life, checking your compass regularly is essential if you want to stay on course. Accordingly, the Compass Check is a tool to be used daily or weekly. Remember this frequency as you create it. Let's begin.

STEP ONE: PRAY

Ask God to superintend the development of your Compass Check and to help you create a tool that helps your family use His Word as a lamp for your feet and a light for your path.

STEP TWO: COLLECT THE FRUITS OF YOUR BRAINSTORMING

You have been given three opportunities to brainstorm some "check-up" and "filter" questions that can help you reach your desired destination in life. Go back and review your Compass

Check questions at the end of Chapter Eight (page 124), Chapter Eleven (page 182), and Chapter Fourteen (page 232). Copy the best of those questions in the space provided below:

Compass Check Questions from Your Brainstorming Sessions

_____

_____

_____

_____

_____

_____

_____

_____

_____

_____

_____

_____

STEP THREE: CONSIDER THE QUESTIONS USED BY OTHERS

In the same way we considered others' responses during the "Rocking Chair" exercise, we believe you will benefit from the wisdom and insight of others as you think about these things.

Below you will find some compass check questions that families have found most helpful in their journeys. Make a mark by those questions you might want to adopt or modify for your own Compass Check.

CHECK-UP QUESTIONS

- ☐ In the last week, have we been experiencing busy or full?
- ☐ Are sports, kids activities, or media causing us to drift off course?
- ☐ Am I living fully present with God and others or distracted and hurried?
- ☐ If I replicate the amount of time I spent with my kids last week, what will they say about our relationship in the rocking chair?
- ☐ Are we scheduling the things that matter most before we schedule everything else?
- ☐ Have I been giving those I care about most my best or my leftovers?
- ☐ Are we treating busyness like we would treat a cobra?
- ☐ In the last week, have we been aiming for good kids or godly kids?
- ☐ How is our "oneness" as a couple?
- ☐ Are we experiencing connection and enjoyment with our kids?
- ☐ Are we consistently taking the steps to be our children's primary teachers about God and His Word?
- ☐ In the last week, have we played, laughed, and learned about God with our kids?
- ☐ Have we been using our tongues to bring life or death to our relationships?
- ☐ Is the foundation of our family life training in godliness?
- ☐ In the last week, is my correction of our children aimed at the heart or the behavior?
- ☐ In the last week, have we been aiming for the American Dream or the Kingdom of God?

☐ In the last week, have we been focused on the hurting, the lost, the poor, and the needy?

☐ What steps are we taking to expand the Kingdom of God?

☐ If we look at our calendar and checkbook, what have we been seeking first?

☐ Are we checking our compass together often enough to impact our choices?

☐ Have we given up on something that we desperately want to be able to say at the end of our lives?

☐ Are we allowing technology to distract us from the most important things?

FILTER QUESTIONS

☐ If every "yes" means a "no," what might this actually cost us?

☐ Would saying "yes" to this fragment our family or bring us together?

☐ Have I checked with my spouse before saying yes to this opportunity?

☐ Does this opportunity/activity line up with the Word of God?

☐ Does this activity build relationships in our family?

☐ Would Jesus watch this movie, read this book, listen to this song with us?

☐ Why are we doing this?

☐ Does this match what God cares about most?

☐ Does this activity/book/movie/song bring us closer to God?

☐ Would doing this lead us more toward the American Dream or the Kingdom of God?

☐ Is this commitment/activity still helping us get where
   God wants to take us?

☐ Will I be happy I said "yes" to this at the end of my life?

STEP FOUR: FINE-TUNING

Review the best questions from your own brainstorming and the questions from others you feel might be worth adding. Evaluate them in light of your answers to the "Rocking Chair" exercise. Which questions will be most effective in helping you arrive at the rocking chair hearing the words you most want to hear?

Do you have a good balance of "check-up" and "filter" questions? Are there questions that help protect you from drifting off course in your most vulnerable areas? Most people feel that a Compass Check between five and ten questions is broad enough to cover the key areas of life and concise enough to employ regularly.

STEP FIVE: LAUNCH

Record your final list of questions using the template below (also available at sonrisemountainranch.org). Select an easily accessible spot for your Compass Check to live. Many families have selected the front of the refrigerator or a five-by-seven-inch frame displayed in a well-lived area of the home.

Once you have completed the first version of your Compass Check, plan a special family night or date night for the inaugural compass check. Dedicate your compass check to the Lord and spend time praying He would use it for His purposes in your life and for the expansion of His Kingdom. Agree on the frequency to check your compass and put it on the family schedule for the next three months.

THE _____ FAMILY COMPASS CHECK

Questions to help you stay on course.

Examples

In the last week, have we been experiencing busy or full?
Does this "yes" fragment our family or bring us together?

_____

_____

_____

_____

_____

_____

_____

_____

_____

_____

_____

_____

_____

_____

_____

_____

_____

_____

Go to sonrisemountainranch.org to download and print this page.

HOW TO USE YOUR COMPASS CHECK

A well-crafted Compass Check can aid in lining up all your choices toward the same target—a destination you will not regret. Using your Compass Check is not rocket science but chiefly an exercise in remembering.

First, when you plan your day, think about your compass check questions to prioritize, filter, and set the right tone. For example, one of my compass check questions is a key daily reminder: "Am I living fully present with God and others, or am I distracted and hurried?"

This question prompts me to remember how the Lord wants me to live and how I want to live every minute. I am careful to not fill my day to the point of overload that would push me toward distraction and hurry. Then, if I encounter some unexpected developments, I am in the best place to adapt as necessary and remain focused on living fully present with everyone around me.

> AM I LIVING FULLY PRESENT WITH GOD AND OTHERS, OR AM I DISTRACTED AND HURRIED?

Second, when you face a choice, reference your compass check questions to determine if one of them sheds light by reminding you of the values you want to guide your choices. For example, I can spend a Saturday afternoon watching a game and putting a lot of value in the outcome or I can go for a walk with my wife and play a board game with my kids.

If I think through my compass check questions, one of them intersects this situation: "Does this activity build relationships in our family?"

This question helps me remember what I want my wife and kids to experience in my relationship with them and I remember that the outcome of the game will be meaningless at the end of my life. The choice is straightforward. When I choose not to watch the game,

I am sometimes tempted to start a pity party over my perceived "sacrifice." In these situations we do well to remember that our Compass Check questions have been prayerfully and thoughtfully selected in light of God and His ways.

The Lord is not keeping you from the best—He is guiding you into the life He designed. Trusting in Him and making choices by referencing what I will care about most at the end of my life delivers the greatest joy day in and day out.

THE BIG IF

Your Compass Check will be valuable and help you stay on course IF:

1. You use it regularly. While you get familiar with the compass check, reading through the questions at the beginning or end of each day is optimal. After you have the Compass Check memorized and have become accustomed to using it, you can make a plan for how often you want to read through the questions.

Most people choose to set a specific time to go through the Compass Check with their spouse or family each week. Keep the "filter" questions close at hand when you or your family has an invitation to do something new.

2. You use it with your family in a way that brings harmony. Undoubtedly, your enemy would like to make the Compass Check a source of division. Stay on guard. Make sure the tone of your conversation is humble, loving, and God-honoring. Including older children into your Compass Check time allows them to see and embrace the values you are trying to live out.

3. You review and update it regularly—perhaps once each year. As a first-time Compass Check user, review your compass check after the first month of putting it to use. Make sure the questions are relevant, effective, and sufficient. Determine if new questions need to be added. Plan to review it annually, or at some regular interval, thereafter. Consider doing this review at the beginning of each school year or around New Year's Day.

4. You use it regularly. This point is worth repeating. The following accounts will help you see why.

A TALE OF TWO FAMILIES

One couple attended a retreat and went home with a well thought out Compass Check and an unprecedented level of excitement. This couple had experienced a decade of turmoil in their marriage and felt this new tool would bring them into a new land of oneness.

Within six months, they had drifted off course farther than ever before and their marriage was on the verge of collapse. Why? They both admitted not using the compass check shortly after returning home. They replicated the choices they had made over the previous ten years even though they "knew better." Because of the unrest at home, this family halted the international adoption process they had recently begun.

Contrast this with another who family attended a retreat, likewise returning home with their Compass Check questions in hand. The husband's involvement in three part-time endeavors had made life a whirlwind and they went home with a commitment to simplify and begin finding areas to invest in the Kingdom. The husband wrote us this a month later:

[My wife] and I have been putting what we learned and discussed into practice in our daily lives. What a difference it has made! Despite a considerable amount of uncertainty

and chaos in our lives right now (possible change of job, trying to sell our house, move, etc), I am embracing what the Lord has for us and feeling some of that illusive peace.

Over the next year they made careful choices, took steps of faith, and saw the Lord provide one job that would meet their needs. With the newly gained margin and energy, they began the adoption process and adopted a baby born to a young unwed couple.

DEFINING MOMENTS

A defining moment is a point in time where a decision is made or an incident occurs that changes the essence or identity of someone or something. Things are never quite the same after a defining moment.

In April 2005, thirty thousand people gathered at Angel Stadium in Anaheim, California to celebrate the 25th anniversary of Saddleback Church. As a response to what God had accomplished in the first quarter century of their meeting, the entire congregation made this declaration before the Lord. It is a great example of a defining moment.

Today I am stepping across the line. I'm tired of waffling and I'm finished with wavering; I've made my choice, the verdict is in and my decision is irrevocable. I'm going God's way. There's no turning back now!

I will live the rest of my life serving God's purposes with God's people on God's planet for God's glory. I will use my life to celebrate His presence, cultivate His character, participate in His family, demonstrate His love, and communicate His word.

Since my past has been forgiven and I have a purpose for living and a home awaiting in heaven, I refuse to waste any more time or energy on shallow living, petty thinking, trivial talking, thoughtless doing, useless regretting, hurtful resenting, or faithless worrying...

I won't be captivated by culture, manipulated by critics, motivated by praise, frustrated by problems, debilitated by temptation or intimidated by the devil. I'll keep running my race with my eyes on the goal, not the sidelines or those running by me. When times get tough, and I get tired, I won't back up, back off, back down, back out or backslide. I'll just keep moving forward by God's grace. I'm Spirit-led, purpose-driven and mission-focused so I cannot be bought, I will not be compromised, and I shall not quit until I finish the race.

I'm a trophy of God's amazing grace so I will be gracious to everyone, grateful for every day, and generous with everything that God entrusts to me.

To my Lord and Savior Jesus Christ, I say: **However, Whenever, Wherever,** *and* **Whatever** *you ask me to do, my answer in advance is yes! Wherever you lead and whatever the cost, I'm ready. Anytime. Anywhere. Anyway.* **Whatever it takes Lord; Whatever it takes!** *I want to be used by you in such a way, that on that final day I'll hear you say, "Well done, thou good and faithful one. Come on in, and let the eternal party begin!"* [3]

Armed with the same attitude, this point in time can be a defining moment in your life. The direction you head from here will determine what your view from the rocking chair looks like. What you are able to honestly say at the end of your life, what others will say about you, the reality of the legacy you leave for all eternity - each of these incomparably important aspects of life will be determined by your choices from this moment forward.

The God of all creation awaits, ready to guide and help you the rest of the way. The psalmist reminds us of His plan:

> *"You hold my right hand. You guide me with Your counsel, leading me to a glorious destiny. Whom have I in heaven but you? I desire You more than anything on earth. My health may fail, and my spirit may grow weak, but God remains the strength of my heart; He is mine forever."*
> —Psalm 73:23-26 (NLT)

Go with God as your guide and your strength. ∎

CHAPTER FIFTEEN REVIEW & SMALL GROUP QUESTIONS

1. The story of KAL Flight 007 provided some important reminders. Which one is most significant to you at this point in your journey?

_____

_____

_____

_____

_____

_____

_____

2. When do you plan to review your Compass Check? Where is the best location to put your Compass Check so you can see it regularly?

_____

_____

_____

_____

3. Re-read your answers to the Rocking Chair exercise. Now, look at your Compass Check questions. How confident are you that regularly reviewing these questions will help you arrive at your intended destination? What concerns do you have?

_____

_____

_____

_____

_____

_____

_____

4. Sharing Compass Check questions with others can be valuable and enjoyable. Consider sharing some of your questions with your family, a close friend, and/or your small group.

_____

_____

_____

_____

_____

_____

5. In addition to sharing your Compass Check with others, selecting a trusted friend (or couple) to check up with you once a month for the first six months as you begin this new habit dramatically increases the probability that you will successfully integrate the Compass Check as part of your life. Which friend(s) would be best to fill this role? (Note: This is a powerful step that I highly recommend if you want this to be a defining moment in your life.)

_____

_____

_____

_____

_____

_____

APPENDIX A: RECOMMENDED RESOURCES

RECOMMENDED STUDY BIBLES

1. NIV Study Bible
2. Life Application Study Bibles
3. ESV Study Bible

RECOMMENDED COMMENTARIES

New Bible Commentary

BOOKS THAT HELP YOU THINK WELL ABOUT BOY/GIRL RELATIONSHIPS

1. *I Kissed Dating Goodbye* by Josh Harris
   This book gives a compelling case as for why dating as the world does it is not biblical or helpful for marriage.

2. *Boy Meets Girl* by Josh Harris
   In this book, Joshua expands on his first book to explain the principles behind having Godly relationships.

3. *Passion and Purity* by Elizabeth Elliot
   Using her own life as an example, Elizabeth provides guidance on submitting one's love life to the authority of the Lord.

4. *When God Writes Your Love Story* by Eric and Elizabeth Ludy
   This book offers an exciting perspective on romantic relationships. They examine the question, "What would it look like to allow the Author of romance to write your love story?"

STUDIES YOU COULD DO AS A SMALL GROUP WITH FRIENDS AND NEIGHBORS

The Art of Marriage by **Family Life**
www.familylife.com/small-group-studies

Homebuilders Studies (**various**) by **Family Life**
www.familylife.com/small-group-studies

APPENDIX B: SONGS TO SING AS A FAMILY

"Speak to one another with psalms, hymns and spiritual songs. Sing and make music in your heart to the Lord, always giving thanks to God the Father for everything, in the name of our Lord Jesus Christ." —Ephesians 5:19-20

1. *I Love You Lord*

2. *Step by Step*

3. *Father, I Adore You*

4. *Love The Lord Your God*

5. *Lord I Lift Your Name on High*

6. *I Surrender All*

7. *Awesome God* (chorus)

8. *Humble Thyself*

9. *What a Mighty God*

10. *Amazing Grace*

11. *Almighty, Most Holy God*

12. *Trust and Obey*

13. *Onward Christian Soldier*

14. *God is Great, God is Good*

15. *How Great is Our God* (chorus)

16. *Here I Am to Worship* (chorus)

17. *King of Kings and Lord of Lords*

18. *Great is Thy Faithfulness* (chorus)

19. *Great I Am* (chorus)

APPENDIX C: BOOKS THAT CAN HELP YOU THINK MORE LIKE CHRIST

1. *God's Smuggler, The Biography of Brother Andrew*

2. *Jesus Freaks: Stories of Those Who Stood For Jesus,* DC Talk

3. *Pilgrim's Progress*, Abridged version

4. *Jotham's Journey, Bartholemew's Passage,* and *Tabitha's Travels* (Nightly devotionals for Advent)

5. *Amon's Adventure* (A nightly devotional for Lent)

6. *First-Century Diaries* by Gene Edwards

7. Biographies from YWAM publishers:
   George Meuller
   Hudson Taylor
   Amy Carmichael
   Gladys Aylward
   Count Zinsendorf
   Clarence Jones
   Cameron Townsend
   Brother Andrew
   Betsy Greene
   Nate Saint
   William Carey
   Eric Liddell

8. *Heroes of the Faith Series*:
   John Bunyan
   Fanny Crosby
   Jim Elliot
   Billy Graham
   David Livingstone
   Martin Luther
   D.L. Moody

Samuel Morris

John Newton

Charles Spurgeon

Corrie Ten Boom

Sojourner Truth

9. *Sister Freaks* by Rebecca Saint James

10. *Missionary Stories with the Millers* by Mildred Martin

11. *10 Boys Who Changed the World* by Irene Howat

12. *10 Boys Who Didn't Give In* by Howat

13. *10 Girls Who Changed the World* by Howat

14. *10 Girls Who Didn't Give In* by Howat

15. *10 Girls Who Made History* by Howat

16. *Heavenly Man* by Brother Yun (older children)

17. *Do Hard Things* by Alex and Brett Harris

18. *The Hiding Place* by Corrie Ten Boom (older children)

19. *How to Ruin Your Life by 40* by Steve Farrar (older children)

20. *Torches of Joy* by John Dekker

21. *Never Say Die: The Story of David Yone Mo and The Myanmar Young Crusaders* by Doug Hsu (older children)

22. *Share Jesus Without Fear* by William Fey

23. *The Way of the Master* by Ray Comfort and Kirk Cameron

24. Lamplighter Book Collection

Audio Theater to Consider

1. Lamplighter Audio Theater

2. Focus on the Family Radio Theater

APPENDIX D: FAMILY MISSION TRIP INFORMATION

ORGANIZATIONS TO CONSIDER

1. International Family Missions (IFM)

2. Greater Europe Missions (GEM)

3. My Life Speaks—Haiti

4. Sonrise Mountain Ranch—trips available for families that have attended a family retreat.

5. Local Church Trips—Many local churches offer trips where families are welcome to attend.

SUGGESTED STEPS TO MOVE AHEAD

1. Gather as a family to pray and ask God to lead each step and to accomplish His purposes through each step. Commit to watch and pray together as a family. Consider keeping a family journal of things you "see" as you consider going on a trip. Commit to pray at each step along the way.

2. Do some research to find out what organizations and trips might be best for your family.

3. Contact the organizations/trip leaders to find out more information about the specific trip(s).

4. Evaluate the viability of the trip that seems best. Consider the time, energy, financial resources, and risk that is involved. Ask together as a family, "Is it worth it?"

Important Note #1

In our experience, God likes to use this step to help us see what is in our hearts and to build our faith. Do not rush this evaluation. Let God convince each one of His will. Trying to press ahead without everyone being "all in" is a precarious move.

Important Note #2

Some friends and extended family may implicitly or explicitly discourage you from going on a trip to a far away place with your children. Each parent needs to ask, "Will the Lord protect my children in a place like this?"

5. If there is oneness that you should go, make the commitment and remember that God will make the most of every opportunity. You are not just going on a 10-day mission trip. With all the trip preparations and processing the trip afterward, it is more like a four- to six-month mission experience that God will likely use in ways that exceed your ideas.

NOTES

CHAPTER 1—THE VIEW FROM THE ROCKING CHAIR

1. Gary Smalley, and John T. Trent. "Dear Daddy." *In The Language of Love.* (New York, NY: Pocket Books, 1991), 16-19.

2. "Notable Quotes from Billy Graham," BGEA:, November 5, 2009. www.billygraham.org/articlepage.asp?ArticleID=1850.

CHAPTER 2—THE LESSON OF THE COMPASS

1. "Ernest Shackleton." Wikipedia. November 09, 2013. Accessed October 12, 2009. en.wikipedia.org/wiki/Ernest_Shackleton.

2. Psalm 119:9, Matthew 4:4 and 7:24-25, James 1:22-25, 2 Timothy 3:16-17.

3. Matthew 7:26-27, James 1:22-24.

4. David W. Woods, Kenneth D. MacTaggart, and Frank O'Brien, "Apollo 11." Flight Journal. April 8, 2009. history.nasa.gov/ap11fj/05day2-mcc.htm.

CHAPTER 3—LIFE IS ABOUT CHOICES

1. Viktor Frankl. *Man's Search for Meaning.* (New York, NY: Simon E. Schuster, 1984). 86.

2. Emily Smith, and Chris Wilson, "Tiki Barber Dumps Pregnant Wife for Hot Blonde." New York Post. April 07, 2010, www.nypost.com/p/news/local/timing_tiki_plays_field_TMZxMDNXxvBbNgVBToZL8O.

CHAPTER 6—ARE WE AIMING FOR BUSY OR FULL?

1. Richard A. Swenson. *Margin; The Overload Syndrome : Learning to Live within Your Limits.* (Colorado Springs, CO: NavPress, 2002). 147-48.

2. Gordon MacDonald, "Leader's Insight," LeadershipJournal.net (3-9-06).

3. Kerby Anderson. "Time and Busyness-Probe Ministries." Time and Busyness-Probe Ministries. Accessed Nov 17, 2011. www.probe.org/site/c.fdKEIMNsEoG/b.4218335/k.AF9C/Time_and_Busyness.htm.

4. James C. Collins. *Good to Great: Why Some Companies Make the Leap—and Others Don't.* (New York, NY: HarperBusiness, 2001). 70.

CHAPTER 7—THE COST OF THE BUSY LIFE

1. Bill Hybels. "The Character Crisis." Preachintoday.com. Accessed December 5, 2010. www.preachingtoday.com/search/?query=Bill+ Hybels+%22the+Character+Crisis%22&searcharea=articles&typ e=&x=-413&y=-407.

2. John Ortberg. "Leadership Journal." Ruthlessly Eliminate Hurry. April 07, 2002. www.christianitytoday.com/le/2002/july-online-only/cln20704.html.

3. Richard A. Swenson. *Margin; The Overload Syndrome : Learning to Live within Your Limits.* (Colorado Springs, CO: NavPress, 2002). 123.

4. Charles Swindoll. "Listen Slowly." Listen Slowly. Accessed November 17, 2011. www.preachingtoday.com/illustrations/2000/january/5665.html.

5. "Cat's in the Cradle." Wikipedia. February 10, 2013. en.wikipedia. org/wiki/Cat's_in_the_Cradle.

6. CAT'S IN THE CRADLE, Words and Music by HARRY CHAPIN and SANDY CHAPIN, © 1974 (Renewed) STORY SONGS, LTD., All Rights Administered by WB MUSIC CORP. All Rights Reserved.

7. "Cat's in the Cradle." Wikipedia. February 10, 2013. en.wikipedia. org/wiki/Cat's_in_the_Cradle.

CHAPTER 8—AIMING FOR FULL

1. Donna Cox. "Re: Thank you". E-mail message to author. March 12, 2010.

CHAPTER 9—ARE WE AIMING FOR GOOD OR GODLY?

1. Allistair Begg. "The Pulpit: Its Powers and Pitfalls." - Resource Center. Accessed March 11, 2013. www.truthforlife.org/resources/sermon/the-pulpit-its-power-pitfalls/.

2. Scott Brown. "Vision Forum Ministries®." The Greatest Untapped Evangelistic Opportunity Before the Modern Church. March 22, 2006. www.visionforumministries.org/issues/uniting_church_ and_family/the_greatest_untapped_evangeli.aspx.

Eric Reed, comp. "Leadership Journal." Leadership Journal, 2012. Accessed March 13, 2013. www.christianitytoday.com/le/2012/winter/youngleavechurch.html.

3. "Cheating Fact Sheet," Cheating Is A Personal Foul," Accessed April 22, 2013, www.glass-castle.com/clients/www-nocheating-org/adcouncil/research/cheatingfactsheet.html.

4. "Suicide Prevention." Centers for Disease Control and Prevention. August 15, 2012. www.cdc.gov/violenceprevention/pub/youth_suicide.html.

   "Teen Depression Statistics." Teen Depression Statistics - Teen Depression. Accessed September 20, 2013. www.teenhelp.com/teen-depression/depression-statistics.html.

   "Substance Abuse & Mental Health Services Administration." Depression Rates Triple between the Ages of 12 and 15 among Adolescent Girls. July 24, 2012. www.samhsa.gov/newsroom/advisories/1207241656.aspx.

5. "Teen Sex Statistics." Teen Sex Statistics—Stats, Teen Sex Facts, & Info on Teen Sex. Accessed September 20, 2013. www.familyfirstaid.org/teen-sex-statistics.html.

   "Office of Adolescent Health." Office of Adolescent Health. September 3, 2013. www.hhs.gov/ash/oah/resources-and-publications/info/parents/just-facts/adolescent-sex.html.

   "Facts on American Teens' Sexual and Reproductive Health." Facts on American Teens' Sexual and Reproductive Health. June 2013. www.guttmacher.org/pubs/FB-ATSRH.html.

6. "Teen Statistics." Relationship Matters: Accessed April 22, 2013. www.canyourel8.com/teen-statistics.

7. Bruce Wilkinson. *The Three Chairs: Experiencing Spiritual Breakthroughs.* (Nashville, TN: LifeWay Press, 1999). 216.

CHAPTER 10—CORE TRAINING FOR GODLY

1. Ephesians 5:25, Colossians 3:13, Malachi 3:3, Romans 8:29, Colossians 3:9-10, Genesis 1:26-27, 2 Corinthians 3:18

2. "Marital Happiness." Childtrends.org. Accessed April 18, 2013, www.childtrends.org/Files/Child_Trends-2011_04_RB_MaritalHappiness.PDF.

3. Vicki Santillano, "The Eyes Have It: How Eye Contact Affects Our Brains," Divine Caroline, last modified February 3, 2011, www.divinecaroline.com/self/self-discovery/eyes-have-it-how-eye-contact-affects-our-brains.

4. Proverbs 1:8, Proverbs 3:1-2, 5-6; Proverbs 6:20-22; Ephesians 6:4.

CHAPTER 11—AIMING FOR GODLY

1. Bob Smithhouser, and Bob Waliszewski. "The Power of the Media." The Power of the Media | Plugged In. 2001. Accessed November 15, 2011. www.pluggedin.com/familyroom/articles/2008/thepowerofthemedia.aspx.

2. Sharon Jayson. "Human Touch May Have Some Healing Properties," USATODAY.com. September 29, 2008, usatoday30.usatoday.com/news/health/2008-09-28-touch-healing_N.htm.

   Amanda Gore. "Stay in Touch." The Joy Project (web log). Accessed March 25, 2013. www.thejoyproject.com/finding-joy/stay-in-touch.

   "How Hugs Are Proven to Help Your Health: Have You Been Hugged Today?" Accessed April 22, 2013, www.sixwise.com/newsletters/06/07/26/how_hugs_are_proven_to_help_your_health_have_you_been_hugged_today.htm.

3. "4 Disciplines of Execution," 4 Disciplines of Execution, Accessed October, 11, 2011, www.franklincovey.com/4dflv/4D_2Vid.html.

CHAPTER 12—ARE WE AIMING FOR THE AMERICAN DREAM OR THE KINGDOM OF GOD?

1. "Brad Pitt." Wikipedia. September 18, 2013. en.wikipedia.org/wiki/Brad_Pitt.

2. Chris Heath. "The Unbearable Bradness of Being." Rolling Stone, October 28, 1999.

3. "Gen Nexters Say Getting Rich Is Their Generation's Top Goal." Pew Research Center RSS. January 7, 2007. www.pewresearch.org/daily-number/gen-nexters-say-getting-rich-is-their-generations-top-goal/.

4. Todd Leopold. "So You Want to Be Famous." CNN. February 19, 2007. www.cnn.com/2007/SHOWBIZ/books/02/19/fame.junkies/index.html?_s=PM:SHOWBIZ.

5. Sharon Jayson. "Generation Y's Goal? Wealth and Fame - USATODAY.com." USA Today. January 10, 2007. www.usatoday.com/news/nation/2007-01-09-gen-y-cover_x.htm.

6. I. Howard Marshall. "Preaching the Kingdom of God." The Expository Times, October 1977, 13.

7. "Gen Nexters Say Getting Rich Is Their Generation's Top Goal." Pew Research Center RSS. January 7, 2007. www.pewresearch.org/daily-number/gen-nexters-say-getting-rich-is-their-generations-top-goal/.

8. Sharon Jayson. "Generation Y's Goal? Wealth and Fame - USATODAY.com." USA Today. January 10, 2007. www.usatoday.com/news/nation/2007-01-09-gen-y-cover_x.htm.

9. Chuck Klosterman. "The Stranger." The New York Times. September 15, 2002. www.nytimes.com/2002/09/15/magazine/the-stranger.html?pagewanted=all.

10. "Preaching Today. " 60 Minutes Producer Looks for Something to Feed His Soul. Accessed November 17, 2011. www.preachingtoday.com/illustrations/2004/september/15527.html.

11. Randy C. Alcorn. *The Treasure Principle: Unlocking the Secret of Joyful Giving.* (Sisters, Oregon: Multnomah Publishers, 2005). 52.

CHAPTER 13—INVESTING IN THE KINGDOM

1. Dallas Willard. *The Great Omission: Recovering Jesus' Essential Teachings on Discipleship.* (San Francisco: Harper San Francisco, 2006). 120-121.

2. Shaw Clifton. "Others." Gainesville:. October 2007. www.uss.salvationarmy.org/uss/www_uss_gainsville.nsf/vw-sublinks/8F329FAE1A4EFBE380257392005BCBD0?openDocument.

CHAPTER 14—AIMING FOR THE KINGDOM OF GOD

1. "Press Centre." UNICEF. Accessed September 20, 2013. www.unicef.org/media/media_45279.html.

CHAPTER 15—YOUR COMPASS CHECK

1. "Korean Air Lines Flight 007." Wikipedia. October 09, 2013. Accessed March 10, 2013. en.wikipedia.org/wiki/Korean_Air_Lines_Flight_007.

2. "Korean Air Lines Flight 007 Transcripts." Wikisource, the Free Online Library. Accessed March 10, 2013. en.wikisource.org/wiki/Korean_Air_Lines_Flight_007_transcripts.

3. Rick Warren. "The Angel Stadium Declaration." The Angel Stadium Declaration. May 12, 2005. www.christianindex.org/1251.article. "This article is printed from the website www.PurposeDriven.com. Copyright 2005 by Rick Warren. Used by permission. All rights reserved.

ABOUT SONRISE MOUNTAIN RANCH

Sonrise Mountain Ranch is a Christ-centered retreat center focused on helping families embrace God's design, deepen their relationships, and invest their lives in the things that matter most. We aim to accomplish this by hosting:

FAMILY RETREATS

We host weeklong family retreats at Sonrise from Memorial Day through Labor Day to help families live in the light of God's design. Guests are encouraged to attend retreats with others that they are walking alongside on the road of life. Retreats are crafted so people will enjoy the richness and experience the impact of "doing life" together.

MARRIAGE RETREATS

We host weekend marriage retreats in the fall, winter, and spring at Sonrise to strengthen marriages that are running on all cylinders or on their last gasp, and anywhere in between.

FAMILY CONFERENCES

In the fall, winter, and spring, we hold family conferences across the country to inspire and equip families and couples.

MISSION TRIPS

We host mission trips as a next step for families that have attended retreats to provide an opportunity to serve the Lord and expand the Kingdom of God together as a family.

PASTOR/MISSIONARY/MINISTRY LEADER GETAWAYS

Also in the fall, winter, and spring, we provide a place for those serving in full-time vocational ministry to rest and rejuvenate.

If you are looking to slow down and deepen your relationship with the Lord, your spouse, and your family, Sonrise Mountain Ranch could be just the place for you.

SONRISE
Mountain Ranch

Visit www.sonrisemountainranch.org to find out more.

When you get to the end of your life, what will you care about most?

Relationships.

Your relationship with God, your spouse, your children, and your close friends. We know these relationships make up what matters most in life. Yet we live in a fast-paced world where developing deep and meaningful relationships is harder than ever.

In this book, we will explore what it looks like to:
- Live the full life, instead of busy
- Raise children who are godly, not just "good kids"
- Build God's Kingdom together as a family, rather than chasing after the American Dream

This book is designed to help you and your family walk through life making thoughtful and intentional choices while focusing daily on what is most important. It is meant to keep you from experiencing regret at the end of your life and lead you instead to a place of gratitude and contentment.

Are you ready?

SONRISE
Mountain Ranch
www.sonrisemountainranch.org

About the author

Matt McGee is the director of Sonrise Mountain Ranch (SMR), a Christian family retreat center in Colorado. After serving as an Air Force pilot for several years, Matt received a Master of Divinity from Denver Seminary. In 2004, Matt and his wife, Chantal, founded SMR where they serve with their six children.

ISBN 978-1-4675-8812-6

90000>

9 781467 588126